COLLECTOR BOOKS
A Division of Schroeder Publishing Co., Inc.

Early wooden case, $100.00.

On the front cover — clockwise, top: Coke placemat, $10.00; wire and metal sign, "Whatever You Do," one of a set, $250.00; Shiloh presentation bottle in box, $35.00; anniversary stem glass, $55.00; reproduced glass holder, $3.00; playing cards from Coke Club, $12.00; set of four glasses in original box, $35.00; wax 75th Anniversary glass, $5.00; Menu Girl tray, $95.00.

On the back cover: All of these items — tray, cards, can, and glass — were issued as a convention gift boxed set at the 1984 Cola Clan Coventions. This set, still in its original box and in NRFB condition, is now valued at $75.00.

Cover design by Beth Summers
Book design by Christen Byrd
Cover photography by Charles R. Lynch

COLLECTOR BOOKS
P.O. Box 3009
Paducah, Kentucky 42002-3009

www.collectorbooks.com

The current values in this book should be used only as a guide. They are not intended to set prices, which vary from one section of the country to another. Auction prices as well as dealer prices vary greatly and are affected by condition as well as demand. Neither the author nor the publisher assumes responsibility for any losses that might be incurred as a result of consulting this guide.

Contents
ICE COLD

DRINK
Coca-Cola
The Pause That Refreshes

This book is dedicated to Payton Goodykoontz, our beautiful little niece. Welcome to the world and the family. We love you.

I would like to extend my sincere thanks to the following people and businesses, without whose help this book would have been impossible.

Earlene Mitchell
c/o Collector Books
P.O. Box 3009
Paducah, KY 42002-3009

One of the nicest ladies you'll ever meet. She has been collecting since the 1960s, and is a constant source of information. She remains a very active collector.

Gary Metz
P.O. Box 18185
Roanoke, VA 24014
540-725-4311
metzauction@cox.net

Gary Metz remains a mainstay in the advertising world. Gary's primary emphasis is on Coca-Cola and a broad spectrum of collectible advertising.

Antiques, Cards and Collectibles
203 Broadway
Paducah, KY 42001
270-443-9797
acc12512@comcast.net

Located in historic downtown Paducah, Kentucky, the old Michael Hardware Store is a great place for an afternoon of browsing. Ray Pelley and his friendly staff offer a full line of antiques and collectibles.

Charlie's Antique Mall
303 Main St., P.O. Box 196
Hazel, KY 42049
270-492-8175
charlies10@aol.com

Located in the historic community of Hazel, Kentucky, on Main Street, this place has it all. The manager, Ray Gough, has some great dealers with a wide variety of antiques and collectibles and some of the friendliest help you'll find. This border-town mall can keep even the pickiest collector busy for the better part of the day.

Riverbend Auction Company
103 South Monroe St.
P.O. Box 800
Alderson, WV 24910

Patrick's Collectibles
612 Roxanne Dr.
Antioch, TN 37013
615-833-4621

If you happen to be around Nashville, Tennessee, during the monthly flea market at the state fairgrounds, be certain to look for Mike and Julie Patrick. They have some of the sharpest advertising pieces you'll ever hope to find. And if Coca-Cola is your field, you won't be able to walk away from the great restored drink machines. Make sure to look them up — you certainly won't be sorry.

Pleasant Hill Antique Mall & Tea Room
315 South Pleasant Hill Rd.
East Peoria, IL 61611
309-694-4040

Bob Johnson and the friendly staff at this mall welcome you for a day of shopping. And it'll take that long to work your way through all the quality antiques and collectibles here. When you get tired, stop and enjoy a rest at the tea room, where you can get some of the best home-cooked food found anywhere. All in all, a great place to shop for your favorite antiques.

Creatures of Habit
406 Broadway
Paducah, KY 42001
270-442-2923

This business will take you back in time with its wonderful array of vintage clothing and advertising. If you are ever in western Kentucky, stop and see Natalya and Jack.

The Illinois Antique Center
308 S.W. Commercial
Peoria, IL 61602
309-673-3354

This is a day-long stop. Dan and Kim have restored an old, very large warehouse overlooking the river in downtown Peoria. It's full of great advertising and collectibles. Stop by and see Dan and Kim and their very friendly staff, and plan on being amazed.

Rare Bird Antique Mall
212 South Main St.
Goodlettsville, TN 37072
615-851-2635

If you find yourself in the greater Nashville area, stop by this collectors' paradise. Jon and Joan Wright have assembled a great case of dealers whose offerings run the gamut of collectible merchandise. So step back into a time when the general store was the place to be, and be prepared to spend some time.

Bill and Helen Mitchell
226 Arendall St.
Henderson, TN 38340
901-989-9302

Bill and Helen have assembled a great variety of advertising with special emphasis on Coca-Cola, and they are always searching for new finds. So if you have anything that fits the bill, give them a call or drop them a letter.

Richard Opfer Auctioneering, Inc.
1919 Greenspring Drive
Timonium, MD 21093
410-252-5035

Richard Opfer Auctioneering, Inc., provides a great variety of antiques and collectibles auctions. Give his friendly staff a call for his next auction catalog.

Wm. Morford
RD #2
Cazenovia, NY 13035
315-662-7625

Wm. Morford has been operating one of the country's better cataloged phone auction businesses for several years. He doesn't list reproductions or repairs that are deceptive in nature. Each catalog usually has a section with items that are for immediate sale. Try out this site and tell him where you got his name and address.

•••If I have omitted anyone who should be here, please be assured it is an oversight on my part and is not intentional.

•••Coca-Cola, an American icon. A perfect example of how to start with a good product and very little else and become one of the largest businesses in the world. The insight, skill, and pure luck of Asa Chandler in bringing Coke to the forefront of the soft drink industry is a story that could fill volumes of books.

We, as collectors of the best-selling soft drink in the world, are lucky the early industry leaders realized the power of advertising. If an item could be placed in front of the American consumer, Coca-Cola found a place for its name and a slogan the public would remember and repeat. The slogan was stroke of genius for sales, and led to a plethora of advertising items. Collectors of Coke have plenty to choose from — calendars, clocks, ice picks, cards, games, toys, match safes, match strikers, cardboard posters, porcelain signs, Coke discs, pencils, school learning materials, etc. The list is almost endless, and the diligent collector can still find good merchandise at reasonable prices.

This book is designed to be a small take-along edition of Coke values. Easy for both the beginner and the advanced collector to use to keep abreast of items and values. Always know your collecting field and be the winner in your field.

Good luck and good hunting.

•••This book is meant only as a guide, and not as the last word on values. It is another tool in the collector's arsenal of information; remember, an informed collector is one who is smiling at the end of the day.

I've attempted to help both the advanced and beginning collector with this book. I don't attempt to set prices on any Coke memorabilia, only to report values. If you're buying, you will no doubt like that sentence. But if you're selling, it won't be as appealing. When you look at the caption, you will see that I have keyed the prices so that you'll know the origin of the value. You'll see the following key symbols throughout this book:

C — a value given to me by a collector(s)

B — a value determined by an auction price (Remember on auction values that two determined bidders can run a price far past fair market value. Likewise, lack of interest will sometimes let a collectible sell for less than it should.)

D — a value determined by a dealer
A — a value determined by the author

Condition will be graded by the following key:

- NOS — refers to new old stock, usually found in a warehouse or store closed for some time
- NRFB — never removed from box
- MIB — absolutely mint, still in the original container
- M — mint condition; however, has been out of the container
- NM — near mint, nothing to detract from display
- EX — excellent; very minor distractions, such as shelf wear, that don't detract from the focal point
- VG — very good, may have light scratches on the edges or back, but nothing to detract from the fact
- G — good, the usual used condition, with scratches and nicks on the item front, but still desirable
- F — fair, some bad detractions
- P — poor; pick it up only because of its rarity or because it's a piece you don't have in your collection

Of course, other factors, such as location, will affect price. Generally speaking, an item with a $100.00 price in my area (the Midwest and the South) may sell in the $150.00 – 175.00 range on the East Coast and in the Northeast, and in the $200.00 – 225.00 range on the West Coast.

How tough is the demand in my area? I'm a longtime collector of items from my hometown of Paducah, Kentucky. Fortunately for me, the city has a very colorful and rich history, with some great memorabilia. Unfortunately for me, there are several die-hard collectors like myself, and among us, we keep the prices artificially high due to the demand for those few items that are always surfacing.

Probably the last consideration of pricing is condition. This is where I find the most problems. If an item in the price guide is labeled as mint at $200.00, and you see one in a store in fair condition at $200.00, it's overpriced. Don't buy it! I've attempted to make sure all of the listings in this book have the condition listed. This should help when it's time to buy or haggle. It's extremely difficult to find a seller and a buyer that agree on an item's value. A buyer shouldn't be hesitant about making an offer, and a seller shouldn't be offended by an offer. Good luck buying, selling, and collecting.

Banner, canvas, "Coca-Cola brings you Edgar Bergen with Charlie McCarthy...," truck mounted, 1950s, 60" x 42", EX, **$1,100.00 B**. Gary Metz.

Banner, canvas, "Drink Coca-Cola from the Bottle through a Straw," with straight-sided bottle at left, 1910, 70" x 16", EX, **$4,000.00 B**. Gary Metz.

Base for crossing guard, cast iron, "Drink Coca-Cola." There are a lot of reproductions of this — most have a different measurement and the lettering is different, so be careful. 21" dia., VG, **$250.00 C**.

••• Baseball scoreboard, cardboard, very heavy stock, advertising panel at top, "Drink...in Bottles 5¢," unusual item, still with good colors, 1930s, 30" x 20", EX, **$1,000.00 B**. Gary Metz.

••• Bottle, cardboard, hobbleskirt bottle with no message, Canadian, 13" x 33", EX, **$475.00 B**. Gary Metz.

••• Bottle, cardboard, "Take Home Enough," flat mount, die-cut bottle in hand, 1952, VG, **$210.00 C**.

••• Bottle, celluloid, "Drink ...Delicious and Refreshing," straight-sided bottle with paper label, 1900s, 6" x 13", VG, **$2,600.00 B**.

Signs

Bottle, celluloid, "Eis-kalt," flat mount, bottle in hand, foreign, 6½" x 16", VG, **$225.00 B**. Gary Metz.

Bottle, metal, "Buvez Coca-Cola," large embossed hobbleskirt bottle, 17¼" x 53", G, **$145.00 C**. Gary Metz.

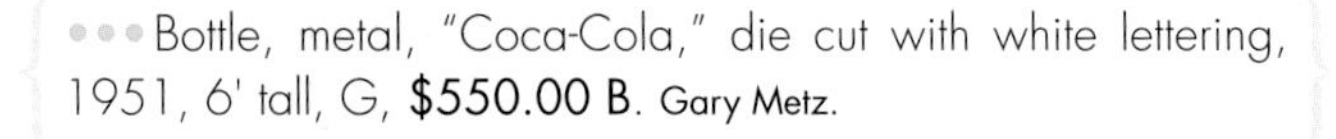

Bottle, metal, "Coca-Cola," die cut with white lettering, 1951, 6' tall, G, **$550.00 B**. Gary Metz.

Bottle, metal, "Coca-Cola...Sign of Good Taste," self framing with fishtail logo and hobbleskirt bottle, 1960s, 31¼" x 11¼", G, **$295.00 C**.

Bottle, metal, "Drink Coca-Cola," flat mount, horizontal, featuring tilted hobbleskirt bottle in yellow spotlight, 1948, 54" x 18", VG, **$395.00 C**.

Bottle, metal, "Drink Coca-Cola," self framing with hobbleskirt bottle to right of message, 1950s, 54" x 18", EX, **$450.00 C**. Eric Reinfield.

Bottle, metal, flat mount, die cut, embossed, 36" tall, G, **$350.00 B**. Gary Metz.

Bottles, cardboard, "Coca-Cola Delicious and Refreshing," flat mount, die cut of six-pack carton, 1954, EX, **$750.00 B**. Gary Metz.

••• Bottle topper, cardboard, "King Size Ice Cold," also has string for use as a hanger or pull, 1960s, **$100.00 – 175.00** C. Joe Wilson.

••• Bottle topper, cardboard, six-pack and food in basket, top hole fits over bottle neck, 1950s, 8" x 7", NM, **$550.00** B.

••• Bottle topper, paper, early cardboard six-pack with only one bottle remaining, 1950s – 1960s, EX, **$10.00 – 15.00** C.

••• Bottle topper, paper, "For Extra Fun Take Mo Than One," 1950s – 1960s, EX, **$15.00 – 20.00**

••• Bottle topper, paper, "Regular Size Coca-Cola" with Santa's elves looking around the carton, 9" x 11¾", EX, **$45.00 – 55.00 C.**

••• Bottle topper, plastic, designed to sit on top of a hobbleskirt bottle, "We Let You See the Bottle," 1950s, EX, **$495.00 – 550.00 C.** Mitchell Collection.

••• Bumper sticker, vinyl, with Max Headroom "Don't Say The 'P' Word," 1980s, EX, **$25.00 C.**

••• Calendar top, paper, pretty girl sitting on a slat-back bench drinking Coke from a straight-sided bottle with a straw, 1913, 16" x 24", G, **$4,500.00 C.**

••• Cash register topper, metal and plastic, "Drink Coca-Cola," 1950s, EX, **$950.00 B**. Gary Metz.

••• Cooler panel insert, metal, "Serve Yourself...Drink Coca-Cola... Please Pay the Clerk," 1931, 31" x 11", G, **$140.00 B – 175.00 C**. Gary Metz.

••• Decal, paper, "Drink Coca-Cola Ice Cold," shield shaped with hobbleskirt bottle, 1934, 18" x 15", EX, **$130.00 B**. Gary Metz.

••• Decal, vinyl, "Drink Coca-Cola...Air Conditioned Inside," 1950 – 1960s, EX, **$15.00 – 20.00 C**.

••• Decal, vinyl, "Drink Coca-Cola... Please Pay Cashier," 1960s, EX, **$30.00 – 40.00 C**.

••• Delivery truck, porcelain, "Drink Coca-Cola Ice Cold," designed for a truck cab, 1950s, 50" x 10", EX, **$350.00 B – 550.00 C**. Gary Metz.

••• Dispenser, stainless steel, "Drink Coca-Cola," horizontal lettering with border trim, 6½" x 3¼", G, **$95.00 B**. Gary Metz.

••• Display, cardboard, "Boy-oh Boy!" 3-D set-up of boy in front of store cooler with a bottle of Coke, 1937, 36" x 34", VG, **$925.00 – 1,100.00 C**. Mitchell Collection.

••• Display, cardboard, cherub holding a tray with a glass of the product, die cut, matted and framed, very rare item, 1908, VG, **$4,000.00 B**. Gary Metz.

••• Display, cardboard, Christmas tree-shaped string hanger with dynamic wave sign, 1970s, 14" x 24", VG, **$40.00 – 65.00 D**.

••• Display, cardboard, clown balancing on a bottle of Coke while holding a 12-pack with one hand and juggling a button on a foot, 1950s, EX, **$875.00 B – 1,200.00 C**. Gary Metz.

••• Display, cardboard, "Coca-Cola...Ice Cold," die cut with diamond can in hand, 1960s, NM, **$230.00 B – 250.00 C**. Gary Metz.

••• Display, cardboard, "Coca-Cola...Ice Cold," featuring a die-cut king-size bottle, 1960s, NM, **$160.00 B – 250.00 C**. Gary Metz.

Display, cardboard, "Beach Robe," "Cool Contrast to a Summer Sun," horizontal, 1940s, 56½" x 21½", EX, **$795.00 C.**

Display, cardboard, die-cut bathing girl in horseshoe, could be used for a window display or wall hanging, matted and framed, 1910s, F, **$1,450.00 B.** Gary Metz.

Display, cardboard, die-cut bell glass of Coke, easel back, snow at base, 1930s, 17" x 27", EX, **$500.00 B – 575.00 C.** Gary Metz.

Display, cardboard, die-cut bottle in hand beside sign, on post that reads "Drink...Delicious and Refreshing," 1900s, 9" x 19", F, **$525.00 – 600.00 C.**

••• Display, cardboard, die-cut boy and girl drinking Coke from a glass through a straw, button in front and "So Refreshing," 1950s, 20" x 13", VG, **$195.00 – 225.00 C**. Gary Metz.

••• Display, cardboard, die-cut boy with dog, sitting on stump and fishing, bottle of Coke in one hand, "Friends for Life," unusual piece, not seen very often, 1935, 36" tall, VG, **$2,650.00 B**. Gary Metz.

••• Display, cardboard, die-cut hobbleskirt bottles, "Every Bottle Sterilized," matted and framed, 1930s, 14" x 12", EX, **$1,300.00 C**.

••• Display, cardboard, die cut of lady with parasol and a straight-sided paper-label bottle, 1900s, 24" x 27", VG, **$5,200.00 B**. Gary Metz.

••• Display, cardboard, die cut of woman holding a six-pack carton, 1940s, 5' tall, EX, **$300.00 – 325.00 C**. Gary Metz.

••• Display, cardboard, die cut of young boy on bicycle, "Have a Coke," 1950s, 29" x 20", G, **$275.00 C**.

••• Display, cardboard, die cut, three ladies at table with Coke, "Be Refreshed," 24" x 18", VG, **$450.00 B**. Gary Metz.

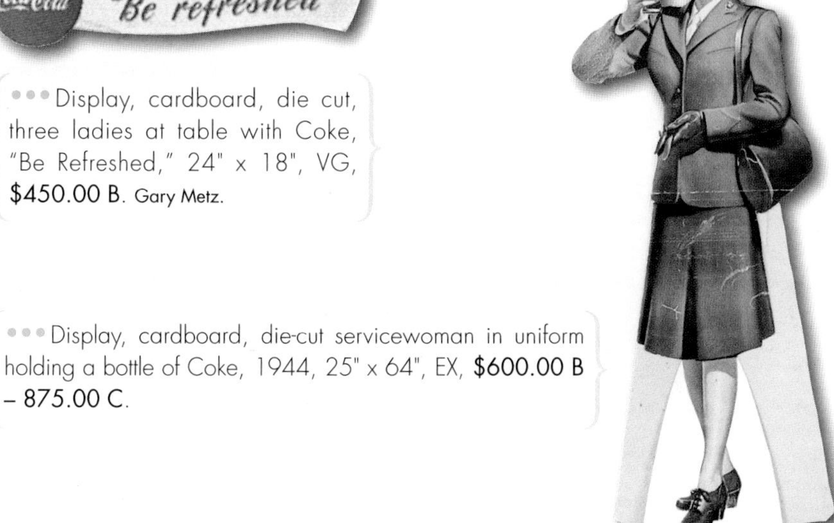

••• Display, cardboard, die-cut servicewoman in uniform holding a bottle of Coke, 1944, 25" x 64", EX, **$600.00 B – 875.00 C**.

••• Display, cardboard, die-cut WWII battleship, matted and under glass, 1940s, 26" x 14", NM, **$1,300.00 B**. Gary Metz.

••• Display, cardboard, die-cut winter girl with glasses of Coke in snow, 1930 – 1940s, 32" x 19", EX, **$695.00 C**.

••• Display, cardboard, "Drink Coca-Cola...Coke Brightens Every Bite," die-cut easel-back standup, 1959, 2' x 3', EX, **$275.00 – 325.00 C**. Gary Metz.

••• Display, cardboard, "Drink Coca-Cola," trifold with cameo center with pretty girl drinking from a flare glass, for window use, 1913, VG, **$5,200.00 B**. Gary Metz.

••• Display, cardboard, "Drink...," die cut of smart teacher rabbit with pointer instructing children sitting on a bench at a school desk, extremely difficult to locate, 1900s, 6½" x 7", NM, **$16,000.00 B**. Gary Metz.

••• Display, cardboard, Eddie Fisher holding a bottle of Coke, cutout with easel back for store use. Note to all the youngsters out there, this was a famous singer in the 1950s. 1954, 5' tall, VG, **$375.00 B – 425.00 C**. Gary Metz.

••• Display, cardboard, "For Extra Fun...Take More Than One," life-size cutout of Jennifer O'Neill with a six-pack carton in each hand, 1960s, 60" x 30", EX, **$130.00 B – 145.00 C**. Gary Metz.

Display, cardboard, "King Size...Ice Cold," commonly known as a fan pull or string hanger, this die cut is double sided and advertises king size Coke, 1950 – 1960s, EX, **$55.00 D – 65.00 C**.

Display, cardboard, "Off to a Fresh Start," die-cut woman wearing a smile and 1920 to 1930s clothing, 1931, 12" x 27", EX, **$875.00 B – 1,000.00 C**. Gary Metz.

Display, cardboard, plastic, "Work Safely," light-up with three work figures carrying a banner that reads, "Work Safety-wise," 1950s, 15½" sq., EX, **$725.00 B**. Gary Metz.

Display, cardboard, ringmaster and assistant die-cut pieces, matted and framed under glass, 1920 – 1930s, 32" tall, EX, **$550.00 – 650.00 C**. Gary Metz.

••• Display, cardboard, "Take Enough Home...2 Convenient Sizes," 1956, 29" x 32", EX, **$525.00 B**. Gary Metz.

••• Display, cardboard, "The Pause That Refreshes" cut out, hard to locate this piece, 1937, 34" x 14", VG, **$200.00 B – 325.00 C**. Gary Metz.

••• Display, cardboard, Toonerville cut-out standups, 14 pieces form a village, G, **$1,900.00 B**. Gary Metz.

••• Display, cardboard, two-piece with two couples having a picnic, "Buy Coca-Cola Now...for Picnic Fun," 1950s, EX, **$135.00 – 185.00 C**. Mitchell Collection.

••• Display, cardboard, waitress cut out holding a tray full of refreshing Coca-Cola, 17" x 20", VG, **$475.00 B**. Gary Metz.

••• Display, cardboard, with boys playing around a real bottle of Coke, Canadian item, very hard to locate, 1930s, 11½" x 11½", EX, **$4,700.00 B**. Gary Metz.

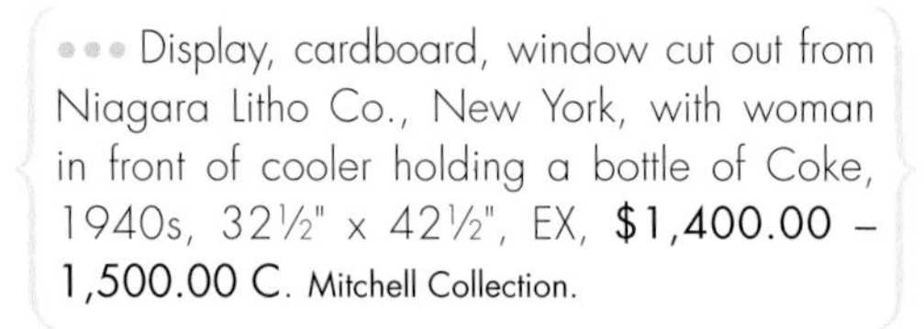

••• Display, cardboard, window cut out from Niagara Litho Co., New York, with woman in front of cooler holding a bottle of Coke, 1940s, 32½" x 42½", EX, **$1,400.00 – 1,500.00 C**. Mitchell Collection.

••• Display, cardboard, woman wearing a hat and sitting on wooden bench and drinking Coke from a bottle, "Coca-Cola in Bottles," 1900s, 18" x 28½", VG, **$8,500.00 C**.

••• Display, glass and plastic, "Drink Coca-Cola...Pause and Refresh" on left side and fan image with bottle in hand on right side, 1940s, 19" x 15½", EX, **$675.00 B**. Gary Metz.

••• Display, glass and plastic, "Drink Coca-Cola...Please Pay Cashier," light-up counter sign with Coke glass at each end, 1950s, 18½" x 8", EX, **$2,600.00 B**. Gary Metz.

••• Display, glass, "Drink Coca-Cola...Please Pay When Served...Thank You," back bar mirror, 1930s, 11" dia., VG, **$650.00 C.** Mitchell Collection.

••• Display, glass mirror, "Drink Carbonated Coca-Cola 5¢ in Bottles," round, G, **$600.00 C.** Mitchell Collection.

••• Display, metal and glass, "Drink Coca-Cola," reverse painting with original chain hanger, chrome frame, 1932, 20" x 12", EX, **$1,500.00 B.** Gary Metz.

••• Display, metal and glass, "Drink Coca-Cola," reverse-painted with original metal frame and chain, 1932, 20" x 12", EX, **$3,500.00 B.** Gary Metz.

••• Display, metal and glass, "Drink ...in Bottles," disc-shaped motion light, 1950, 11½" dia., NM, **$675.00 B**. Gary Metz.

••• Display, metal and glass, "Drink...Sign of Good Taste," disc inside wire circle, 1965, 14" dia., EX, **$400.00 B**. Gary Metz.

••• Display, metal and glass, "Open...," four-sided revolving sign on raised base, light-up, 1960s, 20" tall, NM, **$1,600.00 B**. Gary Metz.

••• Display, metal and glass, "Pause... Drink Coca-Cola...Have a Coke," illusion light behind the word "pause," 1950s, EX, **$925.00 C**. Gary Metz.

••• Display, metal and glass, "Please Pay When Served," light-up counter sign, 1948, 20" x 12", VG, **$2,000.00 C**. Gary Metz.

••• Display, metal and plastic, "Shop Refreshed... Drink Coca-Cola in Bottles... Take Enough Home," light-up with rotating top, 1950s, 21" tall, EX, **$525.00 B**. Gary Metz.

••• Display, metal and plastic, "Drink Coca-Cola," light-up with starburst effect in back of cup, 1960s, 14" x 16", EX, **$575.00 – 600.00 C**.

••• Display, metal and plastic, "Drink Coca-Cola," round illusion light, 1960s, 11" dia., NM, **$775.00 B – 800.00 C**. Gary Metz.

Display, metal and plastic, "Drink Coca-Cola...Thank You...Call Again," double-sided light-up with "Fountain and Prescriptions" on the reverse side, 1950s, 28" x 23", EX, **$1,900.00 B**. Gary Metz.

Display, metal, "Curb Service...Coca-Cola... Sold Here Ice Cold," embossed lettering, driveway sign, 1931, 20" x 28", EX, **$125.00 B**. Gary Metz.

Display, metal, "Drink Coca-Cola," and seven other advertisements on spinning paddles, NOS, 1950s, NM, **$750.00 B**. Gary Metz.

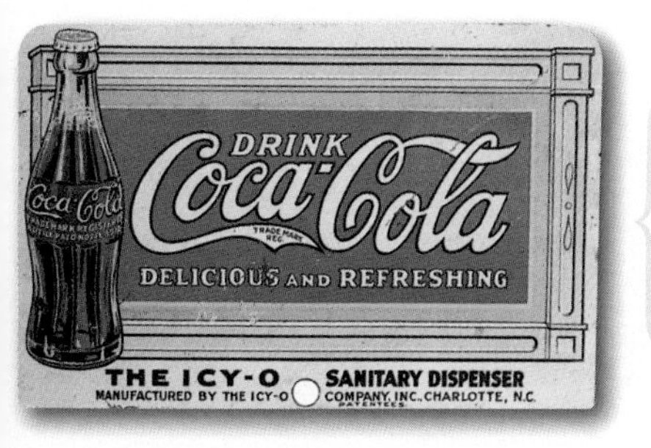

Display, metal, "Drink Coca-Cola, Delicious and Refreshing" by The Icy-O Company, Inc., Charlotte, N.C., hobbleskirt bottle at left of message, EX, **$850.00 B**. Gary Metz.

••• Display, metal, "Gas Today...Drink Coca-Cola While You Wait," with courtesy panel for gas prices, 1929 – 1930, 28" x 20", EX, **$4,500.00 B**. Gary Metz.

••• Display, metal, "Ice Cold...Coca-Cola... Enjoy That Refreshing New Feeling," horizontal, fishtail logo with bottle, 1960s, EX, **$525.00 B**. Gary Metz.

••• Display, metal, "In Any Weather...Drink Coca-Cola in Bottles...Sold Here" on front side with thermometer on left of message, reverse side reads, "Thanks...Call Again," 1930s, EX, **$2,100.00 B**. Gary Metz.

••• Display, neon and metal, "Coca-Cola in Bottles," Art Deco influenced base, rubber feet for counter use, 1950s, EX, **$3,000.00 B – 3,500.00 C**. Gary Metz.

••• Display, neon and metal, "Coke with Ice," nice showy three-color piece, 1980s, EX, **$450.00 – 500.00 C**. Gary Metz.

••• Display, neon and metal, "Drink Coca-Cola in Bottles," with the original crinkle paint, super early piece, influenced by the Art Deco era and difficult to find. Caution: This item has been reproduced; however, the reproduction is very easy to detect. 1939, 17" x 13½", G, **$1,700.00 B – 2,000.00 C**. Gary Metz.

••• Display, neon and metal, "The Official Drink of Summer," a modern multicolored sign, 1989, EX, **$1,100.00 B**. Gary Metz.

••• Display, wood and metal, "Drink Coca-Cola," die-cut wood cooler in center of wire circle with arrow through the cooler, 1940s, 32" x 16", NM, **$550.00 B – 600.00 C**. Gary Metz.

••• Display, wood and metal, "Drink Coca-Cola...Ice Cold" on disc with bottle and arrow, 1939, 17" dia., good, **$450.00 – 550.00 C**.

••• Display, wood, "Coca-Cola" glass being held by pretty blond die-cut woman, 1940s, 42" x 40", VG, **$550.00 B**. Gary Metz.

••• Display, wood, "Drink Coca-Cola," diamond shaped with bottle in yellow spotlight at bottom, 1946, 42" x 42", NM, **$950.00 B**. Gary Metz.

••• Display, wood, "Drink Coca-Cola...Fountain Service" die-cut fountain heads on sides of sign, 1930s – 1940s, 27" x 14", EX, **$1,200.00 B**. Gary Metz.

••• Display, wood, "Drink Coca-Cola...Ice Cold," triangle shaped with arrow pointing down, 1933, EX, **$575.00 B**. Gary Metz.

••• Display, wood, glass, and chrome, "Coca-Cola," plain version of the cash register topper, 1940s, 11½" x 5", good, **$475.00 B – 550.00 C**. Gary Metz.

••• Driveway, metal,"Drink Coca-Cola Refresh," lollipop sign with correct base, 1940 – 1950s, F, **$595.00 D**.

••• Flange, metal, "Drink Coca-Cola... Enjoy That Refreshing New Feeling," horizontal, fishtail design on white background with green stripes, 1963, 18" x 15", EX, **$450.00 B**. Gary Metz.

••• Flange, metal, "Drink Coca-Cola," filigree at top of sign, 1936, 20" x 13", EX, **$700.00 B**. Gary Metz.

••• Flange, metal, "Drink Coca-Cola... Lunch," button at top and arrow mounting "Lunch" message, 1950s, 18" x 22", NM, **$4,000.00 B**. Gary Metz.

••• Flange, metal, "Drink Coca-Cola... Soda," button on top, 1950s, EX, **$3,300.00 B**. Gary Metz.

••• Flange, metal, "Drink Coca-Cola," with bottle in yellow spotlight in lower corner of flange, 1947, 24" x 20", VG, **$625.00 C**.

••• Flange, metal, "Enjoy Coca-Cola in Bottles," round with bottle in circle, 1954, EX, **$4,500.00 B**. Gary Metz.

••• Flange, porcelain, "Coca-Cola...Refresh Yourself...Sold Here, Ice Cold," double-sided shield design, 1930s, 17" x 20", G, **$525.00 B**. Gary Metz.

••• Flange, porcelain, "Iced Coca-Cola Here," 18" x 20", EX, **$775.00 C**.

••• Flat mount, metal and wire, "Drink Coca-Cola... Wherever You Go," beautiful tropical island scene, 1960s, 14" x 18", EX, **$225.00 C**.

Flat mount, metal and wire, "Drink Coca-Cola...Wherever You Go," fishing scene, 1960s, 14" x 18", EX, **$225.00 C**.

Flat mount, metal and wire, "Drink Coca-Cola...Wherever You Go," with saddle on fence, 1960s, 14" x 18", EX, **$225.00 C**.

Flat mount, metal and wire, "Drink Coca-Cola...Wherever You Go," with snow ski scene, 1960s, 14" x 18", EX, **$225.00 C**.

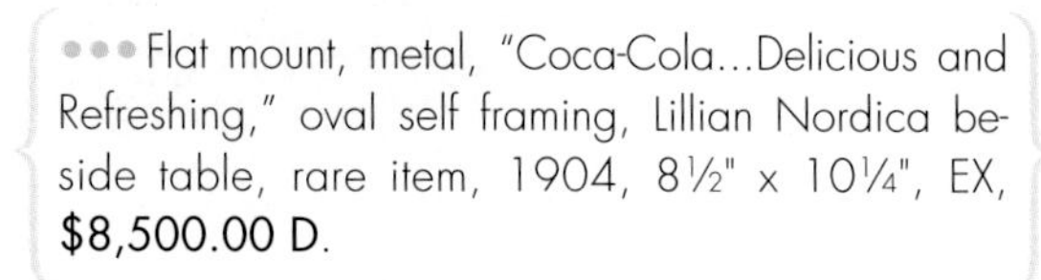

Flat mount, metal, "Coca-Cola...Delicious and Refreshing," oval self framing, Lillian Nordica beside table, rare item, 1904, 8½" x 10¼", EX, **$8,500.00 D**.

••• Flat mount, metal, "Coca-Cola...Delicious and Refreshing...Take a Case Home Today," painted, 19½" x 27¾", VG, **$250.00 D**.

••• Flat mount, metal, "Coca-Cola...Enjoy Big King Size...Ice Cold Here," horizontal, with fishtail design and bottle, 1960s, 28" x 20", G, **$295.00 D**. Gary Metz.

••• Flat mount, metal, "Coca-Cola," Hilda Clark oval, rarely found in the metal version shown here, 1903, 16¼" x 19½", EX, **$3,700.00 B**. Gary Metz.

••• Flat mount, metal, "Coca-Cola...Ice Cold...Sold Here," round with green painted border, 1933, 20" dia., G, **$225.00 B – 275.00 C**. Gary Metz.

••• Flat mount, metal, "Coca-Cola," self framing with fishtail logo, diamond can on right and bottle on left, 1960s, 54" x 18", NM, **$850.00 B**. Gary Metz.

••• Flat mount, metal, "Coca-Cola with Soda 5¢," manufactured by Tuchfarber Co. of Cincinnati, 1902, 17" x 12", G, **$7,200.00 B**. Gary Metz.

••• Flat mount, metal, "Delicatessen," fishtail design with diamond can and bottle, self framing, 1960s, 60" x 24", EX, **$650.00 B**. Gary Metz.

••• Flat mount, metal, die-cut "6 for 25" carton, 1950, 11" x 13", EX, **$775.00 B**. Gary Metz.

●●● Flat mount, metal, die-cut 12-bottle carton, 1954, NM, **$3,000.00 B**. Gary Metz.

●●● Flat mount, metal, die-cut embossed six-bottle pack, "King Size" at top of carton, 1963, 36" x 30", EX, **$725.00 B**. Gary Metz.

●●● Flat mount, metal, die-cut six-pack of bottles with "Regular Size" in yellow spotlight, 1958, 11" x 12", NM, **$1,500.00 B**. Gary Metz.

●●● Flat mount, metal, "Drink Coca-Cola 5¢," Lillian Nordica promoting both fountain and bottle sales, embossed, self framing, 1904 – 1905, EX, **$8,700.00 D**.

••• Flat mount, metal, "Drink Coca-Cola... Delicious and Refreshing." Notice anything different about this sign, which was rejected by Coca-Cola? I included this sign because of the auction interest by collectors, but the "Drink..." message is not in the button but on a somewhat bizarre background, probably a production malfunction. 1954, 18" x 54", EX, **$2,100.00 B**. Gary Metz.

••• Flat mount, metal, "Drink Coca-Cola...Delicious – Refreshing," embossed and painted, with 1923 bottle, 1934, 54" x 30", EX, **$525.00 B**. Gary Metz.

••• Flat mount, metal, "Drink Coca-Cola...Enjoy That Refreshing New Feeling," with fishtail logo and a bottle on striped background, self framing, 1960s, 32" x 12", VG, **$275.00 C**.

••• Flat mount, metal, "Drink Coca-Cola," heavily embossed, with bottle by Dasco, 1931, 4½" x 12½", EX, **$400.00 B**. Buffalo Bay Auctions.

••• Flat mount, metal, "Drink Coca-Cola...Home Cooking Served with a Coke," self framing, horizontal design, 1950s, 50" x 16", EX, **$300.00 B – 350.00 D**. Gary Metz.

••• Flat mount, metal, "Drink Coca-Cola...Ice Cold," embossed, with shadowed 1923 bottle to left of message panel, 1936, 28" x 20", EX, **$850.00 B**. Gary Metz.

••• Flat mount, metal, "Drink Coca-Cola...Ice Cold...Gas...Today... Drink... Sold Here," vertical version, 1936, 18" x 54", G, **$750.00 B**. Gary Metz.

••• Flat mount, metal, "Drink Coca-Cola...Ice Cold," self framing, shadow bottle in vertical design, 1936, 18" x 54", G, **$600.00 B**. Gary Metz.

••• Flat mount, metal, "Drink Coca-Cola...Lunches and Home Made Chili...," green striped background with rolled edges, 1960 – 1970s, 65" x 35", EX, **$235.00 C – 275.00 D**.

••• Flat mount, metal, "Drink Coca-Cola...," oval from McRae Distributors, with pretty redheaded lady, 1910, EX, **$3,650.00 D**.

••• Flat mount, metal, "Drink Coca-Cola...Refresh Yourself...Sold Here Ice Cold," with bottle to right of message, Canadian, 1930s, 28" x 20", G, **$350.00 B**. Gary Metz.

••• Flat mount, metal, "Drink Coca-Cola," self framing, horizontal lettering with bottle in yellow spotlight in lower right- hand corner, 1946, 28" x 20", EX, **$350.00 B**. Gary Metz.

••• Flat mount, metal, "Drink Coca-Cola," self framing, with girl drinking from a bottle of Coke, 1940s, 34" x 12", EX, **$475.00 B**. Gary Metz.

••• Flat mount, metal, "Drink Coca-Cola...Take Home a Carton," self framing, vertical design with yellow spotlight and six-pack carton, 1930s, 18" x 54", G, **$250.00 B**. Gary Metz.

••• Flat mount, metal, "Drink Coca-Cola...Take Home a Carton," six-pack in yellow center spotlight, Canadian, 1940, 36" x 60", G, **$275.00 C**.

••• Flat mount, metal, "Drink Coca-Cola...Take Home a Carton," yellow background seen so often on these Canadian pieces, 1950, 35" x 53", EX, **$625.00 B**. Gary Metz.

••• Flat mount, metal, "Drink Coca-Cola...The Delicious Beverage," known as a turtle sign due to its design, 1920s, 20" x 15", G, **$1,800.00 B**. Gary Metz.

••• Flat mount, metal, "Drink Coca-Cola...Things Go Better With Coke," self framing, courtesy panel at top, 1960s, 60" x 36", good, **$275.00 B**. Gary Metz.

••• Flat mount, metal, "Drink Coca-Cola," unusual "marching" bottles, 1937, 54" x 18", NM, **$800.00 B**. Gary Metz.

••• Flat mount, metal, "Drink Coca-Cola... While You Wait...Gas...Today," 1926, 23½" x 15", G, **$775.00 B**. Gary Metz.

••• Flat mount, metal, "Drink Delicious Refreshing Coca-Cola," Hilda Clark at table with stationary, extremely rare and desirable, 1900s, 20" x 28", EX, **$15,500.00 C**.

••• Flat mount, metal, "Enjoy Coca-Cola...Coke Adds Life to Everything Nice," rolled self-framing edges, 1960s, EX, **$295.00 C**.

••• Flat mount, metal, "Enjoy Coca-Cola," with dynamic wave logo and unusual stripped background, 1970s, 35" x 13", EX, **$125.00 B**. Gary Metz.

••• Flat mount, metal, "Enjoy Coke...Have a Coke and a Smile...Coke Adds Life," painted, with self-framing rolled edges, 1960 – 1970s, EX, **$165.00 C**.

••• Flat mount, metal, "Ice Cold...Prepared by the Bottler of Coca-Cola," vertical, 1960s cup, 1960s, 20" x 28", EX, **$550.00 B**. Gary Metz.

••• Flat mount, metal over cardboard, "Coca-Cola," Chinese, beveled edge, 11" x 8", EX, **$695.00 C**.

••• Flat mount, metal, "Pickup 12...Refreshment for All," 12-pack of bottles in center, self-framing rolled edges, 1960s, 50" x 16", EX, **$595.00 C**.

••• Flat mount, metal, "Taste TAB...Flavor In — Calories Out...A Product of the Coca-Cola Company," self framing with rolled edges, 1960s, 31½" x 12", VG, **$275.00 C**.

••• Flat mount, metal, "Tomese Coca-Cola," embossed painted Spanish kick plate, with straight-sided bottle on each side of message, 1908, 36" x 12", EX, **$2,300.00 B**. Gary Metz.

••• Flat mount, neon and porcelain, "Coca-Cola...Drug Store... Fountain Service," large single-sided sign, 86" x 58" x 8", G, **$3,500.00 B**. Gary Metz.

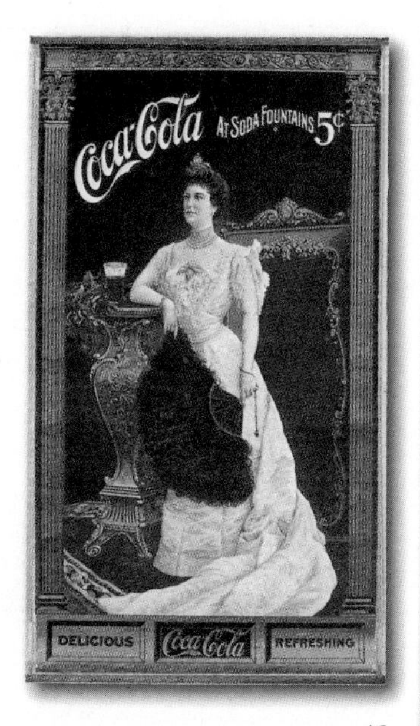

••• Flat mount, oil cloth, "Coca-Cola at Soda Fountains 5¢ Delicious Refreshing," Lillian Nordica holding a large fan beside a table with a glass of Coke, extremely rare. As you can imagine, this item is worth whatever someone with deep pockets is willing to pay. The price I'll give here is the last price I saw this one sell for at auction. 1904, 25" x 47", EX, **$13,000.00 B**.

••• Flat mount, paper, "Drink Coca-Cola...Coca-Cola Brings You Edgar Bergen with Charlie McCarthy...CBS Sunday Evenings," Edgar and Charlie in front of an old CBS microphone, 1949, 22" x 11", EX, **$250.00 C**. Mitchell Collection.

••• Flat mount, paper, "Drink Coca-Cola Delicious and Refreshing," hot dog and hobbleskirt bottle, 1950s, EX, **$195.00 C**. Mitchell Collection.

••• Flat mount, paper, Gibson Girl drinking from a straight-sided bottle with a straw, matted, framed, and under glass, some slight water stains, 1910s, 20" x 30", VG, **$4,600.00 C**. Mitchell Collection.

••• Flat mount, paper, pretty girl with large red bow on white dress drinking from a straight-sided bottle with a straw, matted, framed, and under glass, 1910s, F, **$3,950.00 C**. Mitchell Collection.

••• Flat mount, paper, "Tome Coca-Cola" with swimming star Lupe Velez holding up a bottle of Coke, 1932, 11" x 21", NM, **$1,250.00 C**. Mitchell Collection.

••• Flat mount, porcelain, "Drink Coca-Cola...Delicious and Refreshing...Fountain Service," self framing with design detail on top, 60" x 45½", EX, **$2,400.00 C**.

••• Flat mount, porcelain, "Drink Coca-Cola...Fountain Service," 28" x 12", EX, **$800.00 B**. Gary Metz.

••• Flat mount, porcelain, "Drink Coca-Cola...Fountain Service," Canadian, 1935, 27" x 14", NM, **$1,425.00 D**. Gary Metz.

••• Flat mount, porcelain, "Drink Coca-Cola... Fountain Service," horizontal design, 1950s, 28" x 12", EX, **$700.00 B**. Gary Metz.

••• Flat mount, "Serve...Coca-Cola...at Home," vertical, six-pack in yellow spotlight in center, 1951, 18" x 54", EX, **$350.00 B**.

••• Flat mount, wood and cardboard, "Take Home the New HomeCase...," cardboard case in center spotlight, 1940s, 18" x 48", EX, **$1,600.00 B**. Gary Metz.

••• Hanging, glass, "Please Pay when Served...Coca-Cola," reverse glass, 1950s, 19" x 9½", EX, **$550.00 B**. Gary Metz.

••• Hanging, metal, "Coca-Cola...Sold Here...Ice Cold," die cut, double sided, arrow shaped. Caution: This sign has been heavily reproduced. 1927, 30" x 8", VG, **$450.00 D**.

••• Hanging, metal, "Drink Coca-Cola, Billards," double sided, with hanging brackets, 1934, 63" x 49", EX, **$1,200.00 – 3,500.00 C**. Gary Metz.

••• Hanging, metal, "Drink Coca-Cola...Ice Cold," wrought iron hanging arm, sign has filigree on top, 1937, EX, **$4,000.00 B**. Gary Metz.

•••Hanging, metal, "Rx Drug Rx...Coca-Cola...Store," designed to hang on arm over sidewalk, EX, **$1,300.00 C**.

•••Hanging, porcelain, "Drink Coca-Cola...Delicious and Refreshing...Prescriptions," double sided, "Made in U.S.A. 1933, Tenn Enamel Mfg Co., Nash.," designed to be a sidewalk hanger, 1933, 60½" x 46½", EX, **$1,450.00 C**.

•••Hanging, porcelain, "Drink Coca-Cola," double sided, bottle disc on bottom adds a 3-D effect, 1923, 48" x 60", EX, **$975.00 C**.

•••Hanging, porcelain, "Drink Coca-Cola Ice Cold," single-head fountain dispenser, with metal frame, 28" x 27", G, **$975.00 C**.

••• Hanging, porcelain, "Drink Coca-Cola," very early counter dispenser, 1941, 25" x 26", EX, **$2,200.00 B**. Gary Metz.

••• Kay Displays, flange, wood and metal, "Drink Coca-Cola...Please Pay when Served," bent metal, double sided, 1940 – 1950s, 15" x 12", EX, **$1,250.00 B**. Gary Metz.

••• Kay Displays, wood and brass, "Drink Coca-Cola," filigree at top of shield shaped sign and marching bottles in center, 1940s, 9" x 11", EX, **$525.00 B**. Gary Metz.

••• Kay Displays, wood and chrome, "Drink Coca-Cola...Thirst Asks Nothing More," very scarce item, 38" x 10", G, **$775.00 B**. Gary Metz.

••• Kay Displays, wood and Masonite, "Coca-Cola...Ice Cold," yellow spotlighted bottle at bottom, metal arrow running along back of disc, 1940s, 17" dia., EX, **$2,000.00 B**. Gary Metz.

••• Kay Displays, wood and Masonite, "Drink Coca-Cola Delicious Refreshing," silhouette girl, metal hangers, 1940s, 36" x 14", EX, **$625.00 C**. Gary Metz.

••• Kay Displays, wood and metal, "Drink Coca-Cola," badminton scene, wooden center with wire outside frame, part of a set, 1930 – 1940s, EX, **$425.00 C**.

••• Kay Displays, wood and metal, "Drink Coca-Cola," center displays golfing scene, 1930 – 1940s, EX, **$425.00 C**.

••• Kay displays, wood and metal, "Drink Coca-Cola," die-cut center of United States, disc with glass at bottom, surrounding double metal rings display directions of the compass, unusual item, 1930s, 16" dia., EX, **$1,200.00 B**. Gary Metz.

•••Kay Displays, wood and metal, "Drink Coca-Cola," girl in water with beach ball, 1930 – 1940s, EX, **$425.00 C**.

•••Kay Displays, wood and metal, "Drink Coca-Cola...Pause Here," 1930s, 37" x 10", G, **$1,625.00 D**.

•••Kay Displays, wood and metal, "Drink Coca-Cola," soda glass shield sign, 1930s, 9" x 11½", NM, **$825.00 B**. Gary Metz.

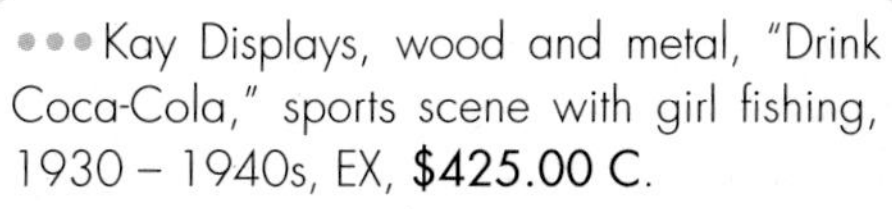
•••Kay Displays, wood and metal, "Drink Coca-Cola," sports scene with girl fishing, 1930 – 1940s, EX, **$425.00 C**.

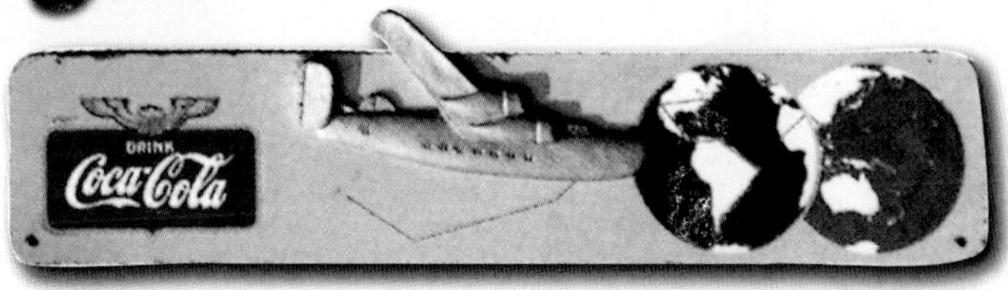

••• Kay Displays, wood, "Drink Coca-Cola," die cut of 1940s-era airplane and both sides of the globe, 1940s, 27" x 7", EX, **$650.00 B**. Gary Metz.

••• Kay Displays, wood, "Drink Coca-Cola," "Work Refreshed," occupational theme with center medallion supporting "Education," 1940s, 23" x 11½", EX, **$375.00 B**. Gary Metz.

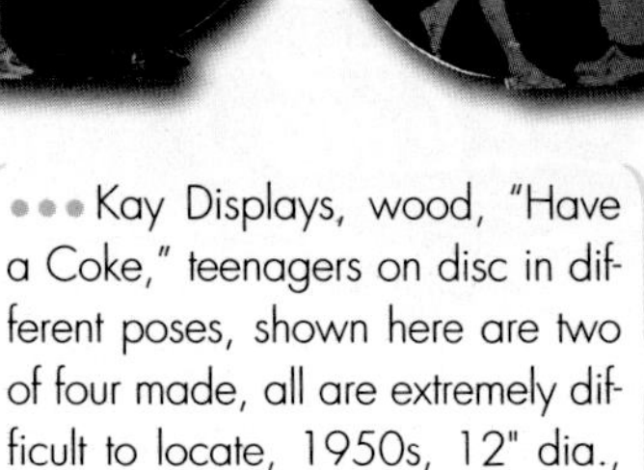

••• Kay Displays, wood, "Have a Coke," teenagers on disc in different poses, shown here are two of four made, all are extremely difficult to locate, 1950s, 12" dia., EX, **$2,200.00 B**. Gary Metz.

••• Kay Displays, wood, "Lunch with Us...A Tasty Sandwich with Coca-Cola," scarce item, 1940s, 9" x 13", EX, **$2,900.00 B**. Gary Metz.

••• Kay Displays, wood, "Please Pay Cashier" medallion with glass at top, 1940s, 13" dia., EX, **$950.00 B**. Gary Metz.

••• Pilaster, metal, "Drink Coca-Cola... Refresh Yourself," unusual version with the "Refresh" top tag, 1950s, 16" x 52", EX, **$1,400.00 B**. Gary Metz.

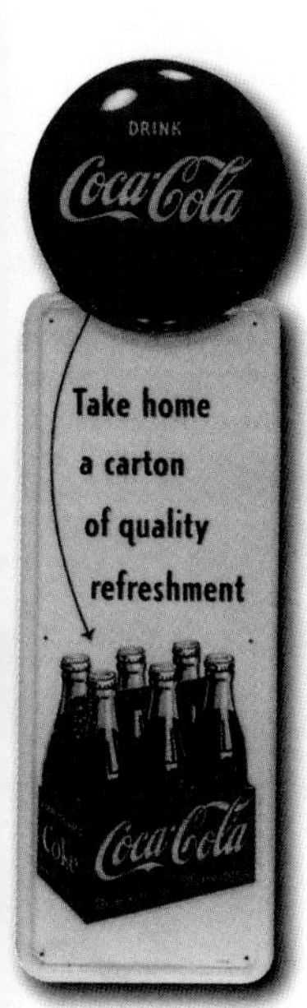

••• Pilaster, metal, "Take Home a Carton of Quality Refreshment," with a cardboard six-pack carton at the bottom, 1950s, 16" x 55", NM, **$875.00 B**. Wm. Morford Investment Grade Collectibles.

••• Poster, cardboard, "All Set at Our House" with young redheaded boy holding a six-pack of Cokes, 1943, EX, **$650.00 B**.

••• Poster, cardboard, "Big Refreshment Value...King Size Coke," pretty lady in wide-brimmed straw hat with bottle of Coke, in metal frame, 1960s, 36" x 20", VG, **$325.00 C.**

••• Poster, cardboard, "Coca-Cola Belongs," military couple at booth, 1930s, 36" x 20", EX, **$1,100.00 B**. Gary Metz.

••• Poster, cardboard, "Coca-Cola," litho of sandwich and bottle of Coke for 35¢, used in lunchrooms and fountains, 1952, 11" x 16", VG, **$225.00 C**.

••• Poster, cardboard, "Coke Belongs," picnickers pulling cold Coke bottles from cooler, back side shows girl at refrigerator, 1950s, 16" x 27", EX, **$900.00 B**. Gary Metz.

••• Poster, cardboard, "Coke Belongs" with young couple sharing a bottle of Coke, 1944, EX, **$700.00 B**. Gary Metz.

••• Poster, cardboard, "Coke for Me, Too," couple with Coke and hot dogs, 1946, 36" x 20", EX, **$450.00 D – 525.00 C**.

••• Poster, cardboard, "Coke Knows No Season," couple in background waving, Coke bottle in gloved hand, with original wooden frame, 1946, 62" x 33", G, **$450.00 C**.

••• Poster, cardboard, "Coke Time," pretty woman in cowboy hat, bottle of Coke, border is surrounded by various cattle brands, 1955, VG, **$375.00 C**.

••• Poster, cardboard, "Cooling Lift," redheaded beauty in pool with a bottle of Coke, 1958, EX, **$500.00 B**. Gary Metz.

••• Poster, cardboard, "Delicious...Refreshing," with Lillian Nordica holding a fan, 1905, F, **$9,300.00 C**.

••• Poster, cardboard, "Drink Coca-Cola 50th Anniversary," with two women sitting on a Coke disc, 1936, 27" x 47", VG, **$1,250.00 B**. Gary Metz.

••• Poster, cardboard, "Drink Coca-Cola...Delicious and Refreshing...Refreshment You Go For," horizontal, with girl on bicycle with front basket full of Cokes, 36" x 20", NM, **$675.00 B**. Gary Metz.

Poster, cardboard, "Drink Coca-Cola...Delicious with Good Food," woman with serving tray full of food and Cokes, Canadian, 1931 – 1932, 18" x 32", EX, **$4,100.00 B**. Gary Metz.

Poster, cardboard, "Drink Coca-Cola," Hostess Girl sitting on the arm of chair and enjoying a bottle of Coke, 1935, 16" x 27", F, **$275.00 C**.

Poster, cardboard, "Drink Coca-Cola...7 Million a Day," vertical, Coke being iced down in metal bucket, 1926, EX, **$850.00 C**.

Poster, cardboard, "Drink Coca-Cola," lady in red outfit with a bottle of Coke, 1940, 30" x 50", EX, **$1,400.00 B**. Gary Metz.

••• Poster, cardboard, "Drink Coca-Cola," vertical bathing beauty, 1940, EX, **$1,200.00 B**. Gary Metz.

••• Poster, cardboard, "Drink Coke in Bottles," three boxers, including Floyd Patterson, 1954, F, **$375.00 B – 450.00 C**. Gary Metz.

••• Poster, cardboard, "Entertain Your Thirst," singer at microphone with a bottle of Coke, 1940s, 36" x 20", EX, **$750.00 C**.

••• Poster, cardboard, "Face Your Job Refreshed," pretty woman at drill press, 1940s, 59" x 30", VG, **$900.00 D**.

••• Poster, cardboard, famous bather from Snyder and Black with round blue background, framed and under glass, considered to be a rare piece, 1938, 22" x 23", EX, **$2,850.00 C**. Mitchell Collection.

••• Poster, cardboard, "For Good Eating," staggered bottles of Coke and food, 1950s, 36" x 20", G, **$295.00 – 350.00 C**.

••• Poster, cardboard, "Have a Coke," bottle of Coke in snowbank, in original wooden frame, 1946, NM, **$550.00 B**. Gary Metz.

••• Poster, cardboard, "Have a Coke," redheaded young lady with a Coke bottle in each hand in front of a drink machine, 1940s, 16" x 27", EX, **$395.00 – 450.00 C**.

••• Poster, cardboard, "Hello Refreshment," horizontal, pretty girl coming out of swimming pool, 1942, 36" x 20", EX, **$1,700.00 B**. Gary Metz.

••• Poster, cardboard, "Hospitality in Your Hands," smiling pretty woman with a tray of Cokes, 1948, EX, **$425.00 B – 575.00 C**. Gary Metz.

••• Poster, cardboard, James Brown, with psychedelic artwork, hard to locate, 1960s, 16" x 27", EX, **$200.00 B – 400.00 C**. Gary Metz.

••• Poster, cardboard, "Let's Watch for 'Em," school girl crossing intersection, 1950s, 66" x 32", NM, **$850.00 B**. Gary Metz.

••• Poster, cardboard, "Mom Knows Her Groceries," girl at refrigerator holding a couple of bottles of Coke, 1946, VG, **$450.00 B – 500.00 C**. Gary Metz.

••• Poster, cardboard, "Nothing Refreshes Like a Coke," couple with bicycles, man in uniform, both enjoying Coke from bottles, 1943, EX, **$1,700.00 B**. Gary Metz.

••• Poster, cardboard, "Play Refreshed," woman with ocean-fishing rod and reel and with a bottle of Coke, 1950s, 36" x 20", VG, **$395.00 – 450.00 C**.

••• Poster, cardboard, "Right Off the Ice," girl at skating rink with a bottle of Coke, 1946, 16" x 27", EX, **$400.00 B**. Gary Metz.

••• Poster, cardboard, "Round the World 1944", die cut lady in heavy coat with a glass of Coke, framed, 1944, EX, **$325.00 D**. Riverside Antique Mall.

••• Poster, cardboard, "Take Some Home Today," young girl in party scene, in original frame, 1950s, 16" x 27", VG, **$675.00 C**.

••• Poster, cardboard, "The Best is Always the Better Buy," girl carrying a bag of groceries and a six-pack carton of Coke, 1943, EX, **$975.00 B**. Gary Metz.

••• Poster, cardboard, "The Drink They All Expect," couple getting ready for guests with bottles of Coca-Cola, 1942, EX, **$700.00 B**. Gary Metz.

••• Poster, cardboard, "The Pause That Refreshes," young lady tennis player being handed a bottle of Coke, vertical version, 1943, EX, **$500.00 B – 550.00 C**. Gary Metz.

••• Poster, cardboard, "They All Want Coca-Cola" waitress with a tray of burgers ordering Cokes, 36" x 20", EX, **$425.00 B**. Gary Metz.

••• Poster cardboard, "Welcome Home," woman reaching for a couple of bottles of Coke and talking to a man in uniform, 1944, 36" x 20", EX, **$450.00 C**.

••• Sidewalk, metal, "Drink Coca-Cola...Ice Cold," fishtail sidewalk sign, 1960s, 22½" x 33", EX, **$500.00 – 625.00 C**.

••• Wall hung, porcelain, "Drug Store...Drink Coca-Cola...Delicious and Refreshing," horizontal and very heavy, 8' x 5', EX, **$1,200.00 D**.

••• Window display, cardboard, "Drink Coca-Cola," with endorsements by Jackie Coogan and Wallace Berry with tall Coke bottle in center, 1934, 43" x 32", EX, **$7,700.00 B**. Gary Metz.

••• Button, metal, bottle decal, hard to find, 1940s, 24" dia., NM, **$400.00 B – 425.00 C**. Gary Metz.

••• Button, metal, "bottle in hand" decal, 1950s, 16" dia., NM, **$250.00 B – 300.00 C**. Gary Metz.

••• Button, metal, "Coca-Cola" with bottle, 1950s, 48" dia, EX, **$600.00 B**. Gary Metz.

••• Button, metal, "Drink Coca-Cola," 1950s, 12" dia., VG, **$150.00 B – 275.00 C**. Gary Metz.

Discs

••• Button, metal, "Drink Coca-Cola" with metal arrow, 1960s, 18" dia., VG, **$775.00 C**.

••• Button, metal, "Standard 6 Bottle Carton," with cardboard six-pack, 1950s, 16" dia., NM, **$425.00 B**. Gary Metz.

••• Display, cardboard, die-cut arrow and disc, layered to make 3-D effect, 1944, 20" x 12", VG, **$195.00 D – 225.00 C**. Gary Metz.

••• Display, metal, "Drink Coca-Cola," round iron frame with button on each side in center, 24" dia., VG, **$1,100.00 C**.

••• Pilaster, metal, "Drink Coca-Cola...Serve Coke at Home," 16" button at top with six-pack carton, 1948, 16" x 54", NM, **$700.00 D**.

••• Sign, Masonite and metal, "Sundaes...Malts," beautiful Kay Displays wings with center 12" button and Sprite Boy and bottle at each end, 1950s, 78" x 12", EX, $1,050.00 B – 1,300.00 C. Gary Metz.

••• Sign, Masonite, "Beverage Department," featuring a "Drink..." button in center of wings that have Sprite Boy on each end, Kay Displays, 1940s, 78" x 12", EX, $850.00 B – 1,000.00 C. Gary Metz.

••• Wall hung, wood and metal, "Drink Coca-Cola" button at bottom, slide menu strips, 1940s, EX, $650.00 B – 775.00 C. Gary Metz.

••• Back bar, cardboard, Autumn Leaves, five pieces, woman with glass of Coke and colorful fall leaves, 1927, good, **$1,000.00 B – 1,200.00 C.** Gary Metz.

••• Back bar, cardboard, "Be Really Refreshed," nine pieces with original envelope and instruction sheet, 1958, 12' long, NM, **$1,600.00 B**. Gary Metz.

••• Back bar, cardboard, "Drink Coca-Cola," framed, under glass, 1918, 96" long, EX, **$4,500.00 B**. Gary Metz.

••• Back bar, cardboard, "Lily Pads," five-piece, great girl in center with a glass of Coke, 1935, EX, **$2,600.00 B – 3,000.00 C**. Gary Metz.

••• Back bar, cardboard, "Verbena," only center pictured, total of five pieces, 1932, EX, **$1,500.00 B**. Gary Metz.

••• Back bar, Masonite, "Howdy Partner," three pieces with the message "...Pause... Refresh," EX, **$850.00 B – 950.00 C**. Gary Metz.

••• Back bar, wood, "Drink Coca-Cola," Kay Displays three-piece with marching Coke glasses, 1930s, 37" x 10" center, 9" x 11½" ends, NM, **$2,800.00 B – 3,000.00 C**. Gary Metz.

••• Back bar, wood, "Drink Coca-Cola," part of a nautical theme unit, 1930 – 1940s, 24" x 13", EX, **$1,400.00 B**. Gary Metz.

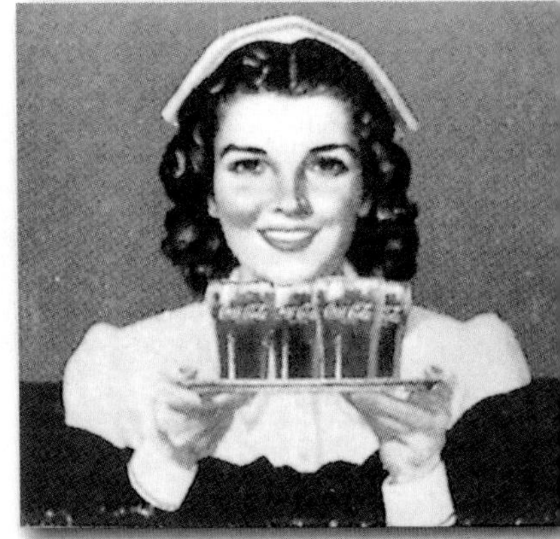

••• Display, wood, waitress and Sprite Boy centerpiece of this festoon, with waitress holding tray with four Coca-Cola glasses, 1946, 37" x 39", EX, **$250.00 B – 300.00 C**. Gary Metz.

••• Desk, metal, "Coca-Cola," perpetual showing month, day, and year, 1920s, EX, **$450.00 C**.

••• Hanging, bamboo, "Drink Coca-Cola in Bottles...Herrin Coca-Cola Bottling Co.," beautiful mountain and stream scene, strong Japanese influence, missing bottom tear sheets, 1920s, VG, **$300.00 – 325.00 C**. Mitchell Collection.

••• Hanging, metal, "Drink Coca-Cola in Bottles" on button on top, 1950s, 8" x 19", EX, **$415.00 B**. Gary Metz.

••• Hanging, paper, Autumn Girl, promoting fountain sales with a glass, partial monthly tear sheets, matted, framed, and under glass, 1921, 12" x 32", NM, **$2,300.00 C.** Mitchell Collection.

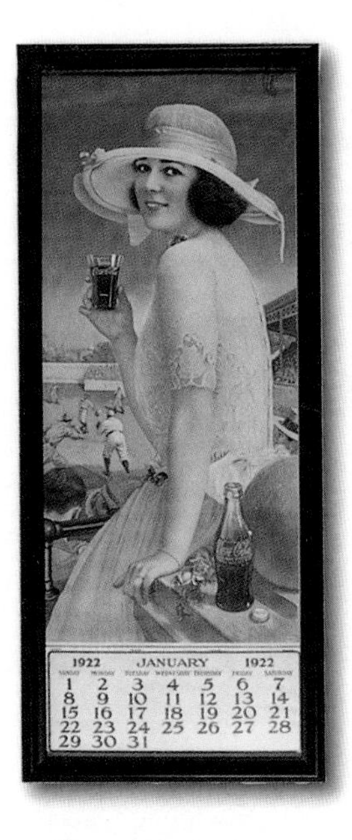

••• Hanging, paper, baseball girl with glass, scene of early baseball game in background, matted, framed, and under glass, 1922, 12" x 32", NM, **$2,200.00 C.** Mitchell Collection.

••• Hanging, paper, "Coca-Cola Bottling Works of Greenwood," scene of scouts in front of Liberty Bell, full monthly tear sheets, 1953, EX, **$500.00 – 550.00 C.** Mitchell Collection.

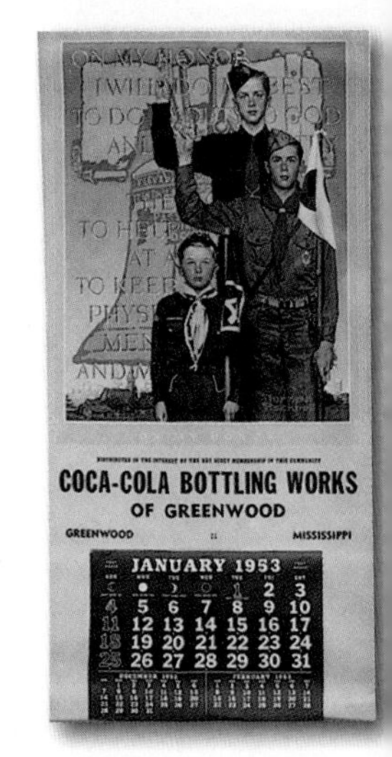

••• Hanging, paper, "Constance" sitting at table with a glass, full pad, matted and framed and under glass, 1917, EX, **$2,700.00 C**. Mitchell Collection.

••• Hanging, paper, "Drink Coca-Cola...Delicious and Refreshing," original metal strip on top, full monthly pad, 1914, VG, **$1,750.00 C**.

••• Hanging, paper, "Drink Coca-Cola Delicious Refreshing," matted, framed, and under glass, 1906, 7" x 15", EX, **$5,300.00 C**.

••• Hanging, paper, Elaine drinking from a straight sided paper label bottle with a straw, partial monthly pad, matted, framed and under glass, 1916, 13" x 32", NM, **$2,200.00 C**.

••• Hanging, paper, Elaine the World War I girl holding a glass, incorrect pad, 1916, 13" x 32", NM, **$2,300.00 C**.

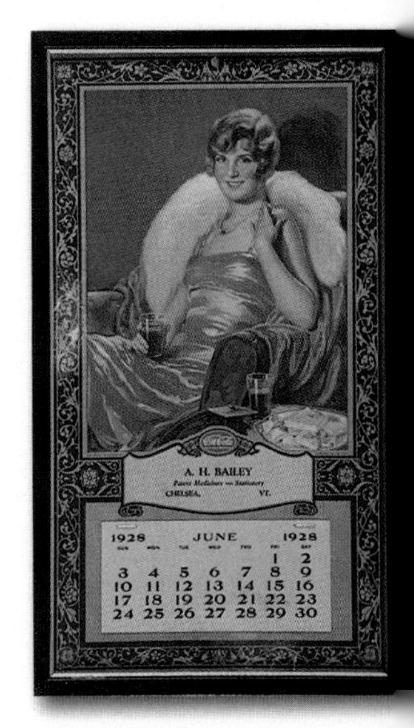

••• Hanging, paper, evening-wear lady holding a glass of Coke, matted, framed and under glass, partial monthly tear sheets, 1928, 12" x 24", M, **$1,100.00 C**. Mitchell Collection.

Hanging, paper, Garden Girl, actually misnamed since the girl is on a golf course holding a glass of Coke, matted, framed, and under glass, 1920, 12" x 32", M, **$2,700.00 C**. Mitchell Collection.

Hanging, paper, girl in coat with a bottle of Coke, double-month display, 1948, EX, **$450.00 – 500.00 C**. Mitchell Collection.

Hanging, paper, girl in sheer dress with a glass of Coke, message panel for Taylor's Billiard Parlor, matted, framed and under glass, 1927, 12" x 24", M, **$1,895.00 C**. Mitchell Collection.

Hanging, paper, girl in tennis outfit with bright red scarf, holding a glass of Coke with a bottle on the table, matted, framed and under glass, 1926, 10" x 18", VG, **$1,195.00 C**. Mitchell Collection.

Hanging, paper, girl in the afternoon, in front of blinds and holding a bottle of Coke, full pad, matted, framed and under glass, 1938, 12" x 24", M, **$775.00 – 800.00 C**. Mitchell Collection.

Hanging, paper; girl smiling, in period dress and holding a glass of Coke while a bottle is sitting on the table; matted, framed, and under glass, beware of reproductions, 1924, 12" x 24", M, **$1,495.00 D**. Mitchell Collection.

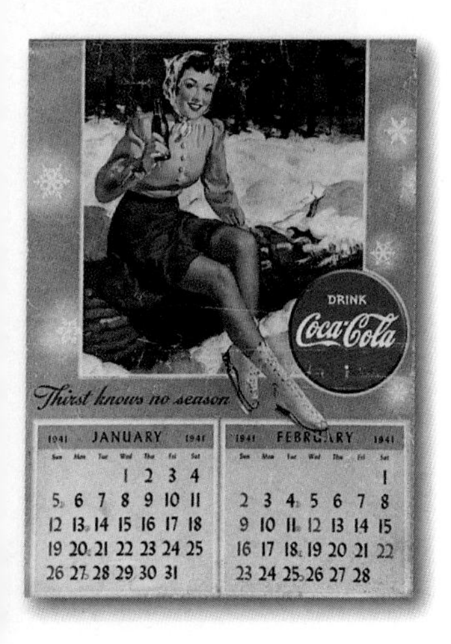

••• Hanging, paper, girl with ice skates and sitting on a log, displays two months at one time, 1941, EX, **$450.00 – 550.00 C**. Mitchell Collection.

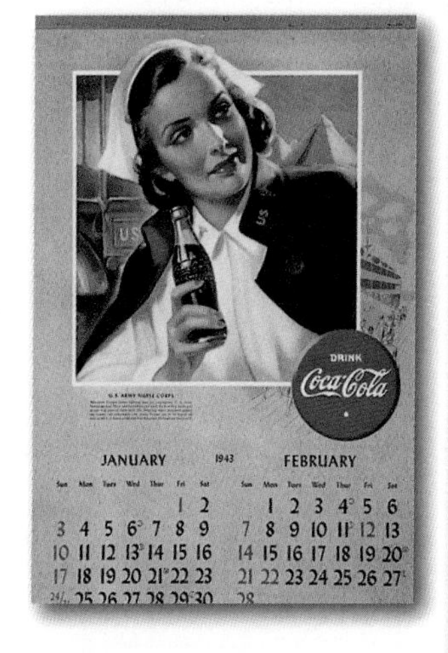

••• Hanging, paper, military nurse with a bottle of Coke, two months shown on each sheet, 1943, EX, **$525.00 – 595.00 C**. Mitchell Collection.

••• Hanging, paper, "Out Fishin'," boy on stump and holding a bottle, full pad, matted, framed and under glass, 1935, 12" x 24", M, **$875.00 C**. Mitchell Collection.

Hanging, paper, party girl with white fox fur around her shoulder and holding a glass of Coke, matted, framed and under glass, 1925, 12" x 24", M, **$1,250.00 C**. Mitchell Collection.

Hanging, paper, southern girl on porch playing music to an elderly gentleman, full pad, matted, framed and under glass, 1934, 12" x 24", M, **$875.00 C**. Mitchell Collection.

Hanging, paper, "The Drink That Makes the Whole World Kin," girl in sheer dress holding a glass of Coke and with a bottle of Coke in an insert panel, matted, framed and under glass, 1927, 12" x 24", M, **$1,200.00 C**. Mitchell Collection.

••• Hanging, paper, village blacksmith with young boy, full pad, matted, framed and under glass, 1933, 12" x 24", M, **$875.00 C**. Mitchell Collection.

Anniversary, metal "75th Anniversary Coca-Cola Bottling Company of Los Angeles," in original box with information booklet, 1977, 10" dia, NM, **$75.00 – 125.00 C**.

Anniversary, metal, "75th Anniversary, Coca-Cola Bottling Works of Jackson, Inc., Jackson, Tennessee," 1980, EX, 12¼" dia., **$5.00 – 10.00 C**.

••• Change receiver, ceramic, "The Ideal Brain Tonic For Headache and Exhaustion...Coca-Cola...," rare item, 1899, EX, **$6,200.00 C**.

••• Serving, metal, "Coca-Cola," couple in early car receiving service at the curb by a soda person, 1927, 13¼" x 10½", VG, **$875.00 C**. Mitchell Collection.

••• Serving, metal, "Coca-Cola," featuring the "Autumn Girl," with a glass of Coke, also on the 1922 calendar, 1925, 10½" x 13¼", EX, **$1,100.00 C**. Mitchell Collection.

Trays

••• Serving, metal, "Coca-Cola," Flapper Girl holding a flare glass with a syrup line, 1923, 10½" x 13¼", EX, **$475.00 – 600.00 C**. Mitchell Collection.

••• Serving, metal, "Coca-Cola is Better — Try It," topless long-haired beauty holding a bottle of Coca-Cola, designed for the bar and tavern trade, distributed by the Western Coca-Cola Company of Chicago without the permission of the home office, 1908, 12¼" dia., EX, **$5,500.00 B**. Gary Metz.

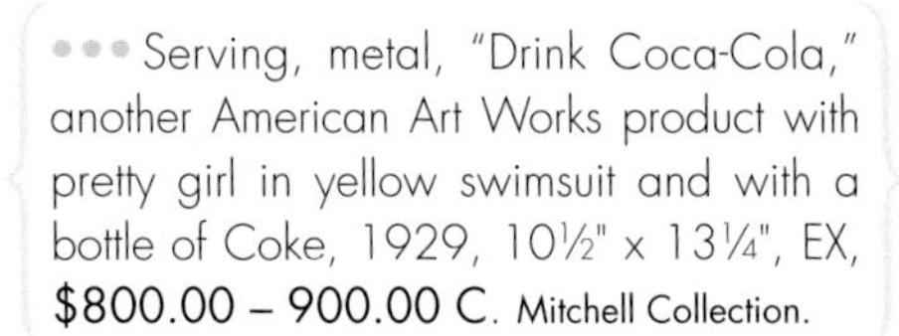

••• Serving, metal, "Drink Coca-Cola," another American Art Works product with pretty girl in yellow swimsuit and with a bottle of Coke, 1929, 10½" x 13¼", EX, **$800.00 – 900.00 C**. Mitchell Collection.

••• Serving, metal, "Drink Coca-Cola," boy and dog at fishing hole eating lunch, 1931, 10½" x 13¼", EX, **$1,100.00 D**. Mitchell Collection.

••• Tip, metal, "Drink Coca-Cola...Delicious... Refreshing," Juanita drinking from a flare glass, 1900s, 4" dia., EX, **$1,075.00 D**.

••• Serving, metal, "Drink Coca-Cola... Delicious... Refreshing," Victorian era with girl with a glass of Coke, round, 1897, 9¼" dia., EX, **$14,000.00 B**.

••• Serving, metal, "Drink Coca-Cola," early golfing couple enjoying Coke, 1926, 10½" x 13¼", EX, **$925.00 C**. Mitchell Collection.

••• Serving, metal, "Drink Coca-Cola," Elaine, also known as the World War I girl with a glass of Coke, made by Stelad Signs Passic Metal Ware Company, Passaic, NJ, 1916, 8½" x 19", EX, **$775.00 C**. Mitchell Collection.

••• Serving, metal, "Drink Coca-Cola," famous Johnny Weissmuller and Maureen O'Sullivan in swimsuits holding Coke in bottles. Caution — this tray has been widely reproduced. 1934, 13¼" x 10½", EX, **$1,100.00 – 1,300.00 C**. Mitchell Collection.

••• Serving, metal, "Drink Coca-Cola," girl in yellow swimsuit running on beach with bottle of Coke in each hand, 1937, 10½" x 13¼", EX, **$425.00 – 500.00 C**. Mitchell Collection.

••• Serving, metal, "Drink Coca-Cola...Have a Coke...Thirst Knows No Season," commonly known as the menu girl, tray was produced in different languages, 1950 – 1960s, 10½" x 13¼", very G, **$95.00 – 135.00 C**. B. J. Summers.

••• Serving, metal, "Drink Coca-Cola...'Meet Me at the Soda Fountain,' " pretty girl on telephone, 1930, 10½" x 13¼", EX, **$600.00 – 650.00 C**. Mitchell Collection.

••• Serving, metal, "Drink Coca-Cola," movie star Madge Evans holding a bottle of Coke and standing beside a chair, 1935, 10½" x 13¼", EX, **$525.00 – 600.00 C**. Mitchell Collection.

Trays

••• Serving, metal, "Drink Coca-Cola," pretty girl in swimsuit in chair on beach with a bottle of Coke, 1932, 10½" x 13¼", EX, **$725.00 C**. Mitchell Collection.

••• Serving, metal, "Drink Coca-Cola," soda attendant with glasses of Coke, 1928, 10½" x 13¼", EX, **$750.00 C**. Mitchell Collection.

••• Serving, metal, "Drink Coca-Cola," St. Louis World's Fair tray with girl at table with a glass of Coke, oval shaped, 1909, 13½" x 16½", EX, **$3,000.00 C**. Mitchell Collection.

••• Serving, metal, "Drink Coca-Cola," two pretty women with Cokes beside a vintage car; due to the demand for metal during WWII, this was the last metal tray produced until the war ended; 1942, 10½" x 13¼", EX, **$500.00 – 600.00 C**. Mitchell Collection.

••• Serving, metal, "Drink Coca-Cola" with flare glass being held up by a pretty young lady, 1907, 10½" x 13¼", EX, **$2,750.00 C**. Mitchell Collection.

••• Serving, metal, "Drink Coca-Cola," woman in white fox fur with glass of Coke, 1921, 10½" x 13¼", EX, **$600.00 C**. Mitchell Collection.

You Are Cordially Invited To The Opening

OF THE NEW HOME OF

Paducah Coca-Cola Bottling Co.

SPECIAL OPEN HOUSE FOR OUR COLORED CUSTOMERS AND FRIENDS WILL BE HELD WEDNESDAY, JUNE 21st

EVERYONE IS INVITED

MUSIC • ENTERTAINMENT • COCA-COLA TO EACH VISITOR

NO CHILDREN ADMITTED UNLESS ACCOMPANIED BY ADULTS

PADUCAH COCA-COLA BOTTLING CO.

BROADWAY AND LA BELLE AVENUE — PADUCAH, KENTUCKY

••• Advertisment, newspaper, full page for the opening of a new bottling plant, 1939, F, $90.00 C. Mitchell Collection.

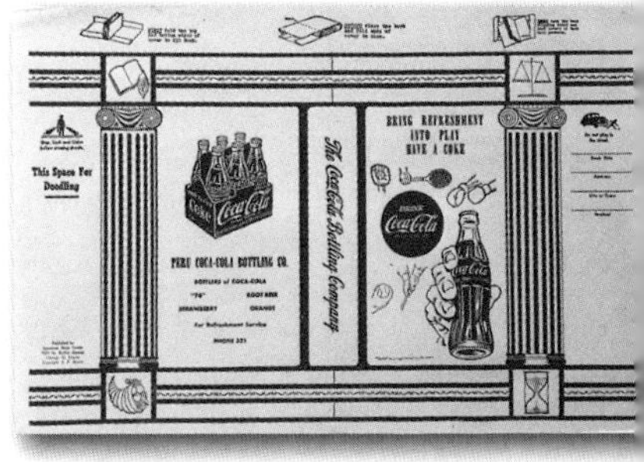

••• Book cover, ***Bring Refreshment into Play Have a Coke***, from the Peru Coca-Cola Bottling Co., 1940 – 1950s, EX, $15.00 C. Mitchell Collection.

••• Book cover, ***Refresh...Add Zest***, front cover has planets and space with rocket blasting off, 1960s, EX, $35.00 – 40.00 C. Mitchell Collection.

Book cover, ***Pause...Refresh, Sign of Good Taste***, wings and hobbleskirt bottles, 1950s, EX, **$10.00 – 12.00 C**.

Book cover, ***Pause...Refresh, Sign of Good Taste***, with cups of Coke, modern art on reverse, 1957, EX, **$15.00 – 18.00 C**.

Check, "Coca-Cola Bottling Co. No. 1" written on the Globe Bank & Trust Co., Paducah, Kentucky, and signed by the owner and bottler, Luther F. Carson, 1908, EX, **$110.00 C**. Mitchell Collection.

Coupon, cardboard, "Enjoy These 6 Bottles with Our Compliments," woman at table with a six-pack carton, 1930 – 1940s, EX, **$10.00 – 15.00 C**. B. J. Summers.

●●● Coupon, cardboard, "Save This Valuable Coupon," 1940 – 1950s, EX, **$8.00 – 10.00 C**. B. J. Summers.

●●● Coupon, "Pause & Refresh...Drink Coca-Cola in Bottles," good for a 5¢ bottle, VG, **$20.00 C**.

●●● Napkin, rice paper, "Drink Coca-Cola, Delicious, Refreshing at Soda Fountains and Carbonated in Bottles," with handwritten note at bottom that reads, "A farewell reception in honor of Mrs. Lucy Stump of New Mexico at the residence of Dr. H. Van Sandt Sat. night Nov 1–1902," framed and matted, 1900s, EX, 14½" x 15" framed size, **$200.00 – 300.00 A**.

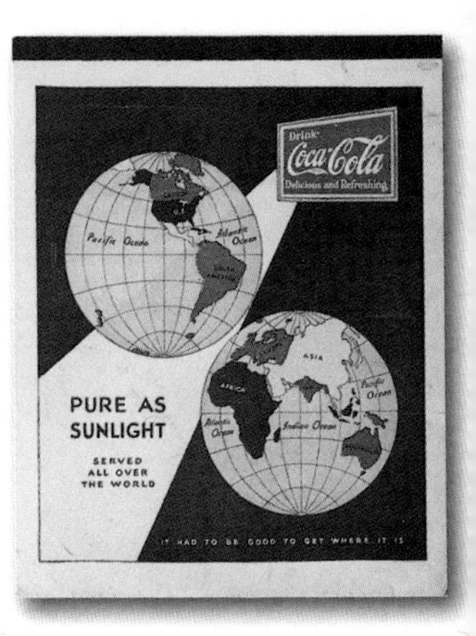

●●● Notebook, "Drink Coca-Cola...Pure as Sunlight," 1930s, VG, **$35.00 C**. Gary Metz.

••• Poster pasted on sheets of paper, "Steel...a Modern Essential," educational items with fantastic colors and material for classroom use, demand seems to be slowly rising on items but is still low in comparison to other Coke advertising, 1940 – 1950s, EX, **$50.00 – 75.00 C**. B. J. Summers.

Poster, "Our America...Future for Electrical Power," great instructional item with good colors and content, but demand for these remains fairly low, making them a good affordable collectible, 1940s, EX, **$35.00 D.** Creatures of Habit.

Poster, "Our America...Iron and Steel" educational item, number three of four in series for school, 1946, EX, **$30.00 C.** Mitchell Collection.

Sheet music, "Rock Me To Sleep Mother" featuring Juanita drinking from a flare glass, 1906, EX, **$895.00 C.** Gary Metz.

••• Bamboo, solid back, church fan donated by the Ruston, Louisiana, Coca-Cola bottler, 1920s, EX, **$145.00 – 155.00 C**. Mitchell Collection.

••• Cardboard, solid back, "Buy by the Carton," from the Memphis, Tennessee, bottler, 1930s, EX, **$195.00 C**.

••• Cardboard, solid back, "Drink Coca-Cola," featuring a yellow spotlighted bottle, wooden handle, 1930s, EX, **$155.00 – 175.00 C**. Mitchell Collection.

Fans

••• Cardboard, solid back, "Drink Coca-Cola" on colored background with yellow spotlighted bottle, wooden handle, 1930s, EX, **$100.00 – 125.00 C**. Mitchell Collection.

••• Cardboard, solid back, "Drink Coca-Cola... Quality Carries On," with bottle in hand shown bursting through paper, wooden handle, 1950s, EX, **$85.00 – 95.00 C**. Mitchell Collection.

••• Cardboard, solid back, "Drink...Coca-Cola...The Pause That Refreshes," with hobbleskirt bottle, from the Martin, Tennessee, bottler, rolled paper handle, 1940 – 1950s, EX, **$125.00 C**. Mitchell Collection.

••• Cardboard, solid back, "Drink Coca-Cola," with dynamic wave logo, wooden handle, from the Coca-Cola Bottling Works of Greenwood, Mississippi, 1960s, EX, **$40.00 C**.

••• Cardboard, "Be Prepared...Be Refreshed," young Boy Scout at box cooler with a couple of Coke bottles. This blotter crosses collectible lines — Coke, Boy Scouts, and coolers — so it will be sought after by more than just Coke collectors. 1940s, M, **$350.00 B**.

••• Cardboard, "Delicious...Wholesome...Refreshing," Canadian piece with ruler marks and protractor, this one is hard to find, 1930s, NM, **$275.00 B**. Gary Metz.

••• Cardboard, "Drink Coca-Cola...Delicious and Refreshing...The Pause That Refreshes," man in striped jacket at table, 1930s, EX, **$45.00 B – 55.00 C**. Gary Metz.

Blotters

Cardboard, "Drink Coca-Cola...Restores Energy...Strengthens the Nerves," 1926, EX, **$145.00 – 195.00 C.**

Cardboard, "Friendliest Drink on Earth," bottle in hand in front of world globe, 1956, 8" x 4", NM, **$50.00 D – 75.00 C.**

Cardboard, "I Think It's Swell," pretty girl looking at a magazine that has a Sprite Boy ad, 1950s, G, **$35.00 C.**

Cardboard, "The Pause That Refreshes...Ok," boy and his dog, boy is seated and enjoying a bottle of Coke and a sandwich, 1930s, NM, **$105.00 D – 135.00 C.** Gary Metz.

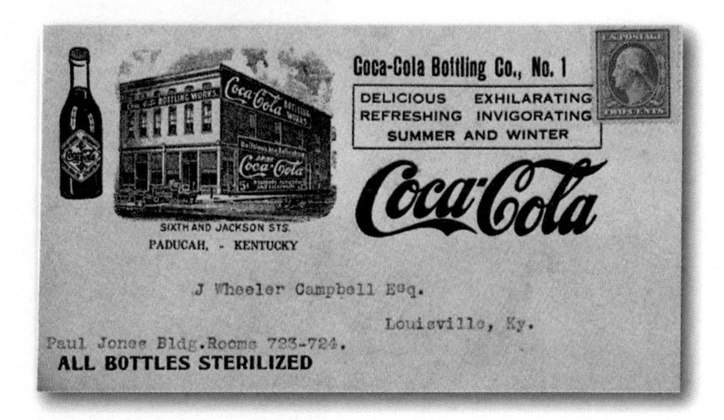

Paper, "Coca-Cola Bottling Co., No. 1," used card with Coke bottling plant. The number 1 on this card refers to the first plant this bottler opened; later he opened and licensed many others. 1920s, EX, $95.00 C – 235.00 B. Mitchell Collection.

Paper, "Coca-Cola...Delicious...Refreshing," scene of Piccadilly Circus, London, with large Coke advertisement on the side of building, EX, $25.00 C. Gary Metz.

••• Paper, "Drink Delicious Coca-Cola," featuring the Hamilton King Coca-Cola girl, 1910, NM, **$775.00 B**. Gary Metz.

••• Paper, "Drink Coca-Cola in Bottles" on door of new International route truck, VG, **$50.00 C**. Mitchell Collection.

Magazine, paper, "Coca-Cola 5¢ Everywhere," front and back cover full page makes one large ad, the ***Housewife***, matted, framed, and under glass, 1910, G, **$190.00 C**.

Magazine, paper, "Drink Coca-Cola...Completely Refreshing," with bathing beauty on towel with a bottle of Coke, 1941, 7" x 10", VG, **$5.00 – 15.00 C**.

Ads

Magazine, paper, "Drink Coca-Cola Delicious and Refreshing," full page back cover of the ***Railway Journal***, glass and bottle of Coke, and an engineer in the cab of an ICRR steam engine, 1929, 8½" x 11", G, $35.00 C.

Magazine, paper, "Drink Coca-Cola," from back page of ***National Geographic***. This is one of the better ads in my opinion; it has a couple projecting the wholesome Coke image, they're in front of a highly sought-after vending machine, the Coke disc (button) is very visible, Sprite Boy is in the image, there is line promoting "Coke Time" with Eddie Fisher on television, and to remind us how good it is, there is the slogan "The Pause That Refreshes...Fifty Million Times a Day." 1955, 7" x 10", VG, $5.00 – 15.00 C.

Magazine, paper, "So Easy to Take Home the Six-bottle Carton," small girl on grocery counter with a vintage cardboard carrier, small black and white insert showing Mom putting the bottles in the fridge to cool, 1949, 7" x 10", VG, $5.00 – 10.00 C.

••• Magazine, paper, "Take Off...Refreshed," pilot and stewardess at airport fountain enjoying a Coke, notice the hanging porcelain sign in the background, 1949, 7" x 10", VG, **$5.00 – 10.00 C.**

••• Magazine, paper, "Thru 50 years...1886 – 1936...The Pause That Refreshes," ladies in appropriate swimwear for the times with bottles of Coke, 1936, 7" x 10", VG, **$8.00 – 12.00 C.**

••• Magazine, paper, "Thru 50 years — Making a Pause Refreshing...Drink Coca-Cola...Delicious and Refreshing," soda fountain attendants of 1886 and 1936, 1936, 7" x 10", VG, **$8.00 – 12.00 C.**

CBS
Drink Coca-Cola
Drink Coca-Cola
YOUR HOST OF THE AIRWAVES
The Coca-Cola Company presents
EDGAR BERGEN with CHARLIE McCARTHY
CBS 8 p. m. EST every Sunday
And every day...wherever you travel, the familiar red cooler is your HOST OF THE HIGHWAYS... HOST TO THE WORKER in office and shop... HOST TO THIRSTY MAIN STREET the country over.

••• Magazine, paper, "Your Host of the Airways," Edgar Bergen and Charlie McCarthy at a box cooler of Coke, 1950, G, **$15.00 C**.

••• Magazine, paper "You Taste Its Quality," from ***National Geographic***, pretty girl drinking from a hobbleskirt bottle, 1951, fair, **$12.00 C**.

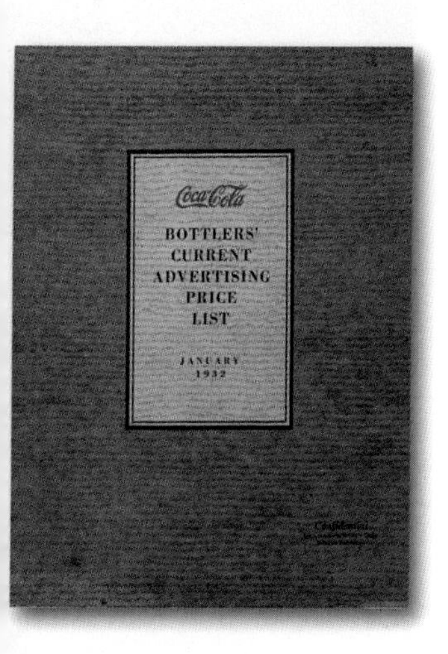

••• 1932 paper, bottlers' current prices for advertising items, EX, **$250.00 C**. Mitchell Collection.

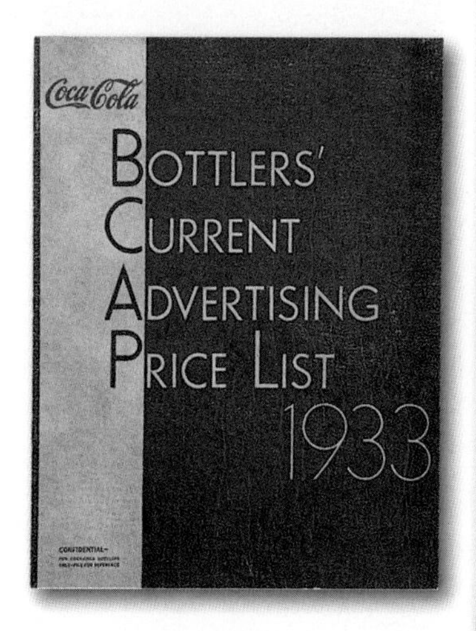

••• 1933 bottlers' price list for Coke advertising items, EX, **$250.00 B**. Gary Metz.

••• 1935 price list for dealers' advertising items, EX, **$235.00 B**. Gary Metz.

••• 1936 paper, 50th anniversary price list for bottlers, EX, **$350.00 B**. Gary Metz.

••• 1944 bottlers' price guide for advertising items, EX, **$275.00 B**. Gary Metz.

••• Installation manual, paper and vinyl, three-ring binder with information about installing fountain stations, 1970s, NM, **$215.00 C**.

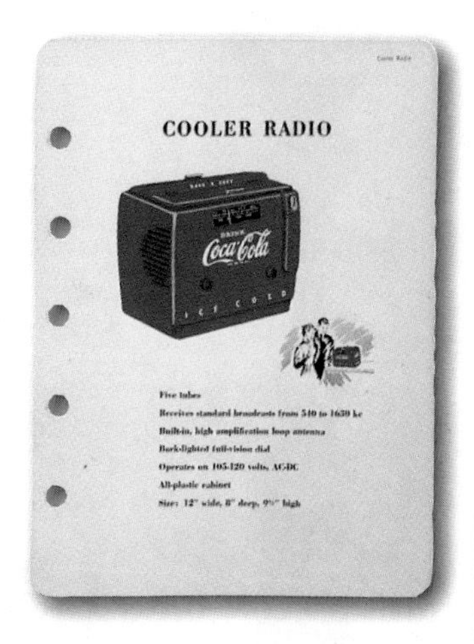
COOLER RADIO

Five tubes
Receives standard broadcasts from 540 to 1630 kc
Built-in, high amplification loop antenna
Back-lighted full-vision dial
Operates on 105-120 volts, AC-DC
All-plastic cabinet
Size: 12" wide, 8" deep, 9½" high

••• Material information, heavy paper stock for five-ring binder with information on the Cooler Radio, 1950s, EX, **$80.00 C**. Mitchell Collection.

••• Paul Flum supply catalog of items needed for advertising, point of purchase to molded fiberglass cooler in shape of older cooler, EX, **$75.00 C**.

••• Carbonation tester, metal, used before the days of premix to determine if the carbonation level was correct, EX, **$725.00 D**.

••• Display, plastic, "Coca-Cola," large hobbleskirt store attention getter, 1953, 20" high, EX, **$375.00 B**. Wm. Morford Investment Grade Collectibles.

••• Hobbleskirt, commemorative, glass, "Root" reissue of the original 1915 bottle, the reissue is marked on the bottom, but the originals were not marked, only 5,000 made, clear, 1965, EX, **$495.00 C**. Mitchell Collection.

••• Hobbleskirt, glass, no return, early generation, full, never opened, 1968, 10 oz., EX, **$10.00 – 12.00 C**.

••• Hobbleskirt, glass, no return, early generation but with screw-off lid, 1960 – 1970s, 10 oz., VG, **$5.00 – 10.00 C**.

••• Hobbleskirt, glass, tall display model of the Christmas 1923 bottle, in original display box with the original tag around the neck of the bottle with instructions for filling, clear, 1930s, 20" tall, EX, **$750.00 B – 850.00 C**. Gary Metz.

••• Hobbleskirt, glass, twist lid, French Canadian, EX, **$5.00 – 10.00 C**.

••• Hobbleskirt, rubber, advertising display piece, 1940s, 43" tall, G, **$850.00 B**. Gary Metz.

••• Jug, stoneware, "Coca-Cola," with paper label, 1910, ½ gal., VG, **$4,300.00 B**. Gary Metz.

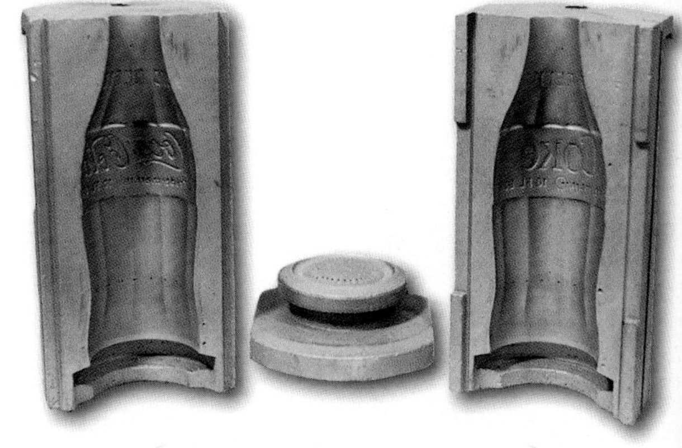

••• Mold, hobbleskirt, iron, made for the 10 oz. no-return bottle, EX, **$525.00 – 575.00 C**.

••• Premix test bottle, with metal casing, glass, 1920s, 7¾" h, EX, **$100.00 – 135.00 C**.

••• Premix test bottle, with wood casing, glass, 1920s, 7¾" h, EX, **$100.00 – 150.00 C**.

••• Seltzer, glass and metal, "Coca-Cola Bottling Company, Bradford, PA," acid etched, light aqua, EX, **$285.00 – 325.00 C**.

••• Seltzer, glass, "Coca-Cola Bottling Company... Cairo, Illinois." Another great example of a Cairo bottle, and contrary to most thinking, this one is scarcer than the Ritz Boy Cairo seltzer. Some calcium deposit on inside of bottle that could be cleaned, and a good clean metal top. 1940 – 1950s, EX, **$575.00 C**. B. J. Summers.

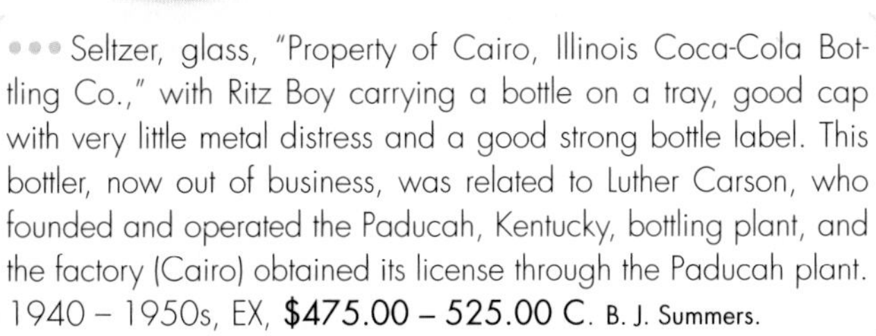

••• Seltzer, glass, "Property of Cairo, Illinois Coca-Cola Bottling Co.," with Ritz Boy carrying a bottle on a tray, good cap with very little metal distress and a good strong bottle label. This bottler, now out of business, was related to Luther Carson, who founded and operated the Paducah, Kentucky, bottling plant, and the factory (Cairo) obtained its license through the Paducah plant. 1940 – 1950s, EX, **$475.00 – 525.00 C**. B. J. Summers.

●●● Straight sided, glass, Biedenharm Candy Co., Vicksburg, Mississippi, lettering arranged in slug-plate fashion on body of bottle, aqua, 1900s, EX, **$450.00 C – 950.00 C.**

●●● Straight sided, glass, block print in circle on front of bottle from Sedalia, Missouri, aqua, 6½", EX, **$65.00 C.**

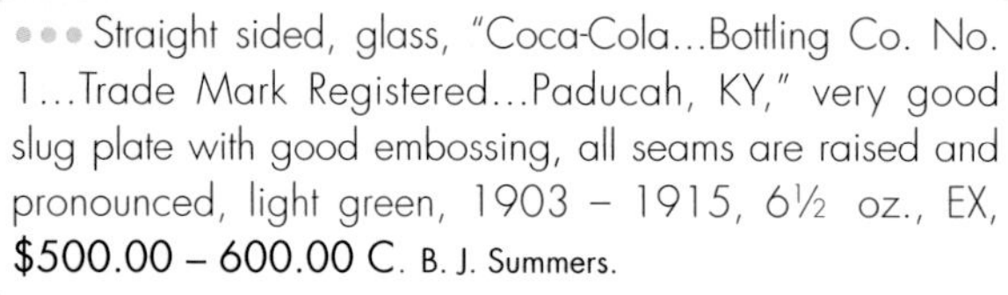

●●● Straight sided, glass, "Coca-Cola...Bottling Co. No. 1...Trade Mark Registered...Paducah, KY," very good slug plate with good embossing, all seams are raised and pronounced, light green, 1903 – 1915, 6½ oz., EX, **$500.00 – 600.00 C.** B. J. Summers.

●●● Straight sided, glass, "Coca-Cola" in script embossed in center with embossed border, aqua, 1910s, 6 oz., VG, **$175.00 – 225.00 C.**

••• Straight sided, glass, "Coca-Cola" in script inside of double diamonds, from Toledo, Ohio, light amber, 1900 – 1910, 6 oz., EX, **$195.00 – 245.00 C**.

••• Straight sided, glass, "Coca-Cola" inside arrow circle, Louisville, Kentucky, light amber, 1910s, 6 oz., EX, **$225.00 – 350.00 C**.

••• Straight sided, glass, "Coca-Cola" on bottom edge of base, "This bottle our private property and protected by registration under Senate Bill No. 130 approved June 7th, 1911," Dayton, Ohio, light amber, 1900 – 1910, 6 oz., EX, **$375.00 – 1,500.00 C**.

••• Straight sided, glass, "Coca-Cola" on front, no location listed, medium amber, 1910s, 6 oz., EX, **$135.00 – 215.00 C**.

Straight sided, glass, first generation throw-away bottle with embossed diamond, inside is embossed bottle and block "Coke," still full, clear, 1960s, 10 oz., NM, **$45.00 – 75.00 C**.

Straight sided, glass, "Registered... Coca-Cola...Bottling Co...To Be Returned to Paducah, KY," clear, 1903 – 1915, 6½ oz., EX, **$175.00 B – 245.00 C**. B. J. Summers.

Syrup, glass, "Drink Coca-Cola" inside etched wreath, metal cap, 1910s, EX, **$700.00 – 1,000.00 C**.

Tab, straight side, glass, early generation, embossed, "Tab, Flavored Dietary Beverage," 1968, 10 oz., NM, **$15.00 – 18.00 C**.

Tab, straight side, glass, first generation embossed bottle, full, never opened, clear, 1960s, 10 oz., NM, **$10.00 – 15.00 C**.

••• "3 Dale Earnhardt," full, 8 oz., 1998, EX, **$6.00 – 10.00 C**.

••• "10 Ricky Rudd," full, 8 oz., 1998, EX, **$5.00 – 8.00 C**.

••• "44 Kyle Petty," full, 8 oz., 1998, EX, **$5.00 – 8.00 C**.

"10 Years, Great Smoky Mountain Railway," full, 8 oz., 1998, EX, **$5.00 – 8.00 C**.

75th Anniversary, "Coca-Cola Bottling Company of Louisville," 1901 – 1976, never opened, 1976, 10 oz., EX, **$8.00 – 12.00 C**.

75th Anniversary, straight sided, "75 years of bottled refreshment, Staunton Coca-Cola Bottling Works, Inc.," 1908 – 1983, never opened, 1983, 10 oz., NM, **$10.00 – 15.00 D**.

75th Anniversary, straight sided, "Alabama Coca-Cola Bottling Company," 1903 – 1978, never opened, 1978, 10 oz., EX, **$12.00 – 15.00 C**.

••• 75th Anniversary, straight sided, "First 'Bottler's Contract' for Coca-Cola, Nashville, 1900 – 1975," never opened, 1975, 10 oz., NM, **$15.00 – 20.00 A**.

••• 75th Anniversary, "The Atlanta Coca-Cola Bottling Company, 1900 – 1975," full, never opened, 1975, 10 oz., NM, **$4.00 – 8.00 C**.

••• 75th Anniversary, straight sided, "The Coca-Cola Bottling Company of Chicago, 1901 – 1976," never opened, 1976, 10 oz., NM, **$8.00 – 15.00 C**.

••• 75th Anniversary, straight sided, "The Coca-Cola Bottling Works Co., Cincinnati, Ohio," 1901 – 1976, never opened, 1976, 10 oz., EX, **$4.00 – 8.00 C**.

••• 75th Anniversary, straight sided with painted facsimile of paper label, clear, 1978, 10 oz., EX, **$15.00 – 20.00 C**.

••• 75th National Convention anniversary, straight sided, Hutchison-style bottle, fairly difficult to locate, light aqua, 1961, EX, **$295.00 – 350.00 C**.

••• 75th Anniversary, straight sided, "World's 1st Coca-Cola Bottling Company Chattanooga, 1899 – 1974." never opened, 1974, NM, **$15.00 – 20.00 C**.

••• "100th Biedenharn Vicksburg Coca-Cola, 1894 – 1994, First Bottler of Coca-Cola," never opened, 1994, 8 oz., NM, **$8.00 – 12.00 D**.

•••"100 Years of Trust, 1901 – 2001, Walgreen's," full, 8 oz., 2001, EX, **$8.00 – 12.00 C**.

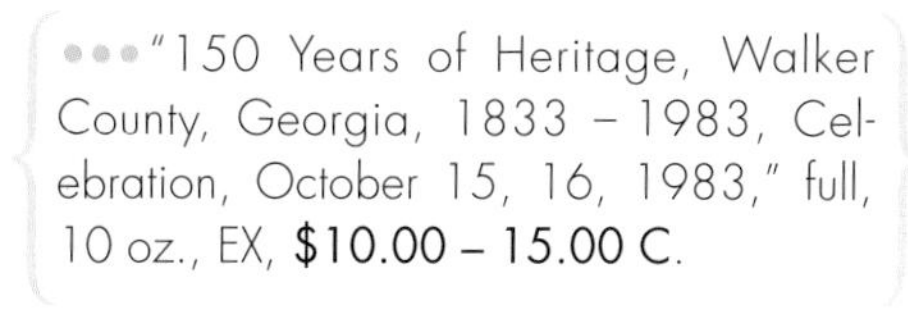

•••"150 Years of Heritage, Walker County, Georgia, 1833 – 1983, Celebration, October 15, 16, 1983," full, 10 oz., EX, **$10.00 – 15.00 C**.

•••"Albertville 92," full, 8 oz., 1992, EX, **$8.00 – 10.00 C**.

•••"Coca-Cola, Sri Lanka," International Christmas bottle, full, 6½ oz., EX, 1990, **$15.00 – 25.00 C**.

"The Cola Clan...Mid South," straight sided bottle for the third annual Septemberfest in Elizabethtown, KY, clear, 1979, 10 oz., EX, **$30.00 C**.

"The Cola Clan, 9th Annual National Cola Clan Convention, August 3 – 6, 1983, Washington, D.C.," full, 10 oz., 1983, EX, **$35.00 – 45.00 C**.

"Congratulations Class of 2002," full, 8 oz., 2002, EX, **$5.00 – 8.00 C**.

"The Grand Dome Room Chattanooga Choo-Choo, Centennial," "Coke and Choo-Choo on the Right Track," full, 10 oz., 1980, EX, **$15.00 – 20.00 C**.

●●● "Judge Isaac C. Parker, 1838 – 1896 Celebrating 100 Years of Law & Order, Fort Smith, Arkansas," 1996, 8 oz., EX, **$8.00 – 12.00 C.**

●●● "New Orleans, 1996 Mardi Gras," full, 8 oz., 1995, EX, **$10.00 – 12.00 C.**

●●● "Publix, Where Shopping Is a Pleasure 1930 – 1980," full, 16 oz., 1980, EX, **$20.00 – 30.00 C.**

●●● "Schmidt's Marvelous Museum, The Memorabilia of Coca-Cola Special Preview Showing the Cola Clan Second Annual Convention Coca-Cola Bottling Company, Elizabethtown, Kentucky, August 6, 1976," 10 oz., EX, **$15.00 – 20.00 C.**

••• Shiloh National Military Park 100th Anniversary, in original box with information sheet, 1894 – 1994, EX, **$35.00 C**.

••• Super Bowl 2000, in original carton, 2000, 8 oz., NM, **$95.00 C**.

••• "The University of Mississippi, Sesquicentennial 1848 – 1998," 8 oz., all six-full bottles in original cardboard six pack, 1997, EX, **$50.00 – 60.00 C**.

••• Contour, metal, with hobbleskirt bottle on outside, produced to feel like a hobbleskirt bottle, trial issue that didn't work, 1990s, 12 oz., EX, **$9.00 C**.

••• Diamond, metal, full-length diamond with bottle in center of diamond, 12 oz., EX, **$110.00 D – 135.00 B**.

••• Dynamic wave, waxed paper, "Coca-Cola" on front, prototype that was never put into production, metal top and bottom, 12 oz., EX, **$175.00 C**.

••• Straight sided, metal, paper label syrup can, red and white, 1940s, 1 gal., EX, **$350.00 D**.

••• Bell, glass, anniversary, presented to John W. Boucher, 1936, NM, **$375.00 B**. Gary Metz.

••• Bell, pewter, "Coca-Cola," scarce, 1930s, EX, **$375.00 B**. Gary Metz.

••• "Celebrating Coca-Cola and Sports, Drink Coca-Cola, Springtime in Atlanta, April 12 – 14, 1990," produced by Belcrest, Inc. Clifton, New Jersey, under authority of the Coca-Cola Co., all four glasses still in original box, 1987, EX, 15 oz., **$28.00 – 35.00 C**.

••• Convention glass, "Coke & Music, Springtime in Atlanta, March 20 – 23, 2002," with dancing couple on 45rpm record, "Enjoy that refreshing new feeling," on reverse side, 2002, 8¼" high, EX, **$8.00 – 15.00 A**.

••• Flare, glass, "Drink Coca-Cola," etched syrup line, clear, 1910s, EX, **$500.00 C**. Mitchell Collection.

••• Glass and holder, glass is new with syrup line and holder is new with 1985 date on bottom, 1980s, EX, **$30.00 C**.

Glass holder, "Coca-Cola," silver, 1900, VG, **$2,400.00 B**. Gary Metz.

Olympic glass, various nations on front, 1976, EX, 5¼" h, **$9.00 – 12.00 C**.

Shot glass, "Refreshes you Best," EX, **$4.00 – 5.00 C**.

World's Fair, glass with scene of Knoxville during the 82 World's Fair, EX, **$4.00 – 6.00 C**.

China

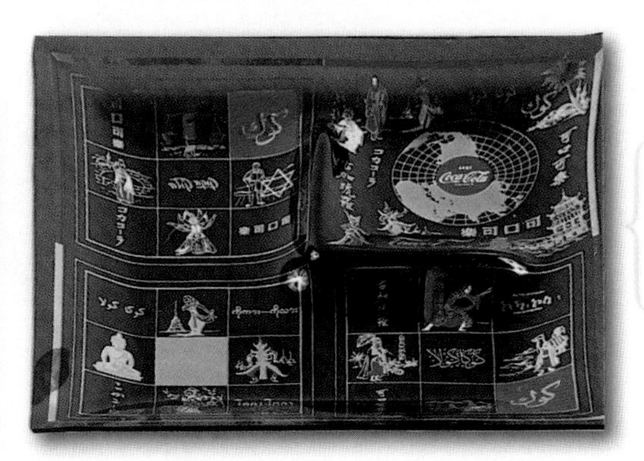

Nut dish, "Coca-Cola," different world scenes, 1960s, 11½" x 11½", EX, **$145.00 C**.

Sandwich plate, "Drink Coca-Cola... Refresh Yourself," bottle and glass in center, 1930s, 8¼" dia., NM, **$1,200.00 B**. Gary Metz.

Sandwich plate, "Drink Coca-Cola... Refresh Yourself," bottle and glass in center, Knowles China Co., 1931, 8¼" dia., NM, **$775.00 B – 850.00 C**. Gary Metz.

••• Metal, Western Coca-Cola Bottling Co., dark-haired lady with a very low drape pose, 1908 – 1912, 9⅞" dia., 16" sq. in frame, EX, **$450.00 – 500.00 C**.

••• Metal, Western Coca-Cola Bottling Co., pretty brunette with rose, back of plate is marked with the bottler information, 1905, EX, 10", **$450.00 B – 595.00 C**. Buffalo Bay Auction Co.

••• Metal, Western Coca-Cola Bottling Co., topless long-haired beauty, this is the one everyone is after, a very popular plate, double the value shown if the original shadow box is still with the plate, 1908 – 1912, 9⅞" dia., 16" sq. in frame, EX, **$1,200.00 – 1,500.00 C**.

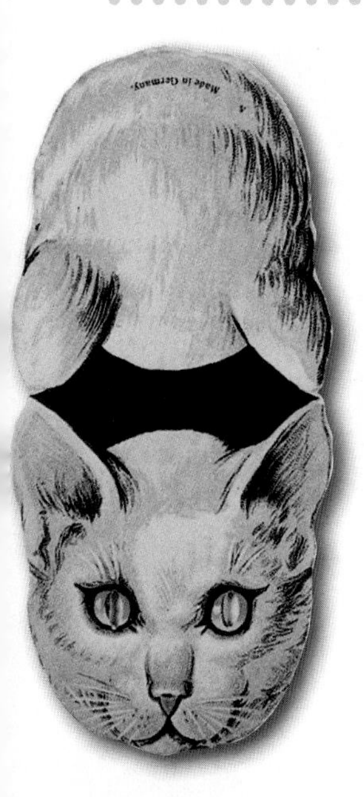

••• Pocket, cardboard, "Drink Coca-Cola in Bottles," folding in shape of cat's head, 1920s, EX, **$895.00 C**. Mitchell Collection.

••• Wall, glass and metal, "Drink Coca-Cola in Bottles," silhouette girl at bottom and thermometer on left side, 1939, 10" x 14¼", VG, **$850.00 B**. Gary Metz.

Thermometers

Wall, metal and glass, "Drink Coca-Cola in Bottles," round dial type reading, 1950s, 12" dia, EX, **$250.00 B – 285.00 C**. Gary Metz.

Wall, metal and plastic, "Things Go Better with Coke," round Pam with dial-type scale reading, 1950s, 12" dia., NM, **$250.00 B – 300.00 C**. Gary Metz.

Wall, metal, Coca-Cola bottle in oval background, 1938, 6¾" x 16", EX, **$350.00 – 400.00 C**. Mitchell Collection.

●●● Wall, metal, "Drink Coca-Cola...Be Really Refreshed," round dial with fishtail logo in center, 1959, 12" dia., NM, **$600.00 B**. Gary Metz.

●●● Wall, metal, "Drink Coca-Cola Delicious and Refreshing," silhouette girl at bottom of scale, 1930s, 6½" x 16", EX, **$500.00 C**. Beware of reproductions. Mitchell Collection.

●●● Wall, metal, "Drink Coca-Cola," die-cut double-bottle gold version, 1942, 7" x 16", EX, **$525.00 – 600.00 C**. Beware of reproductions. Mitchell Collection.

Thermometers

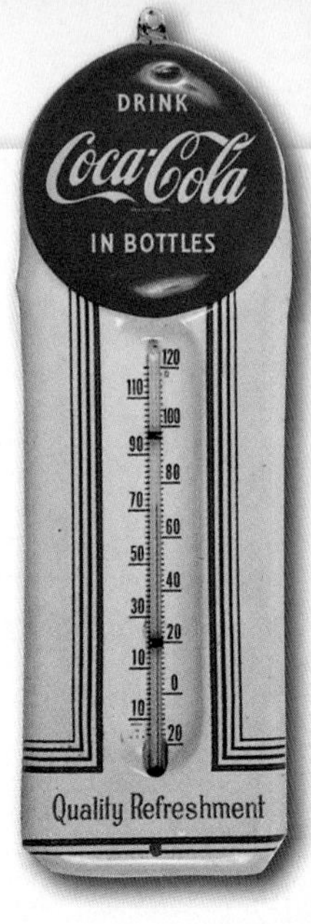

••• Wall, metal, "Drink Coca-Cola in Bottles...Quality Refreshment," button at top and scale-type reading, 1950s, EX, **$325.00 – 375.00 C**. Mitchell Collection.

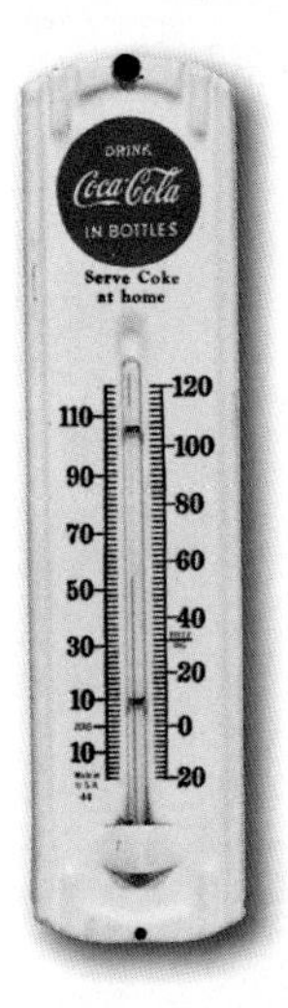

••• Wall, metal, "Drink Coca-Cola in Bottles...Serve Coke at Home," embossed with Art Deco styling, 1948, 9" tall, EX, **$165.00 – 200.00 C**.

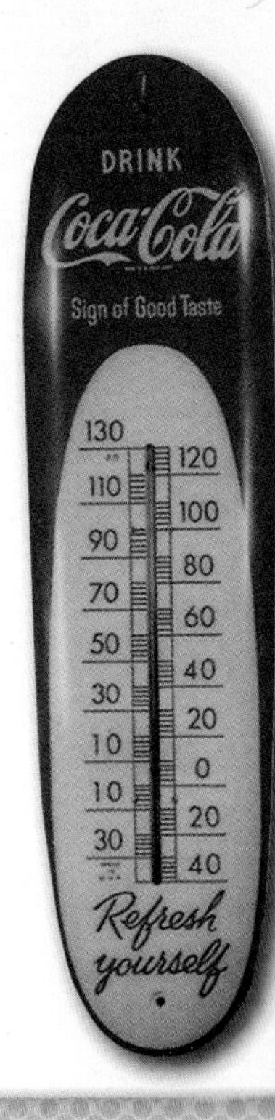

••• Wall, metal, "Drink Coca-Cola...Sign of Good Taste," known as the cigar thermometer due to the shape, good working scale, red and white, 1950s, 8" x 30", EX, **$575.00 B**. Wm. Morford Investment Grade Collectibles.

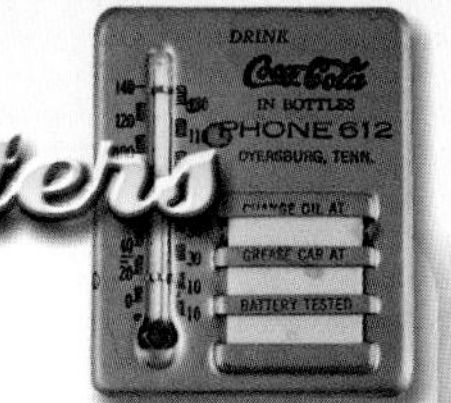

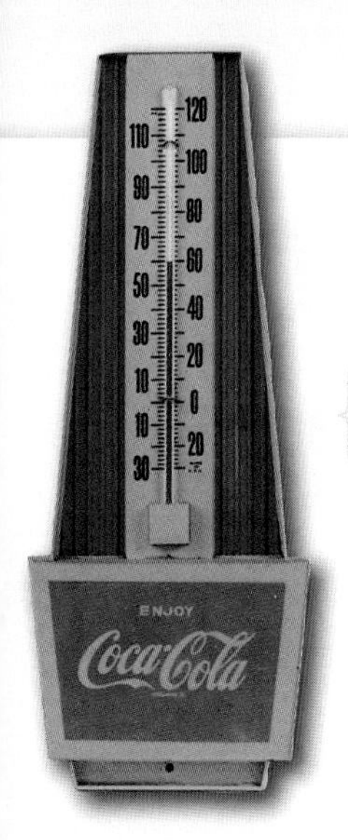

••• Wall, plastic, "Enjoy Coca-Cola," with vertical scale, message panel at bottom, 1960s, 7" x 18", G, **$45.00 C**.

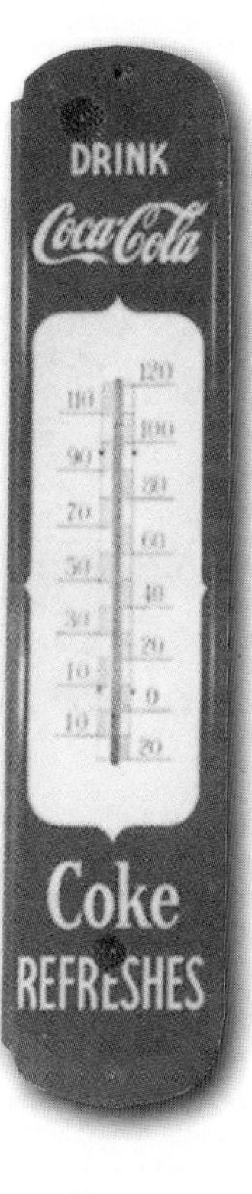

••• Wall, porcelain, "Drink Coca-Cola...Coke Refreshes," vertical scale in center, 1940s, 8" x 36", F, **$750.00 B**. Gary Metz.

••• Wall, wooden, "Drink Coca-Cola in Bottles...," vertical scale, from V. O. Colson Co., Paris, Illinois, 1910s, VG, **$725.00 – 800.00 C**. Mitchell Collection.

Case, 24-bottle, wood, "Refresh Yourself...Drink Coca-Cola in Bottles," very early case with dovetailed joints, 1920s, EX, **$295.00 C**.

Case, wooden, 12 bottle container, VG, **$45.00 – 55.00 A**.

Case, wooden, "Drink Coca-Cola in Bottles, Paducah, KY," 1900s – 1910s, EX, **$75.00 – 125.00 A**. B. J. Summers.

••• Crate, metal, shipping, 48 individual bottle holders, hard to find, "Clifton Forge, VA, Ice & Bottling Works" embossed on front, "Coca-Cola" embossed on lid, 1900s, 22" x 16" x 8¼", G, **$650.00 A – 850.00 C**.

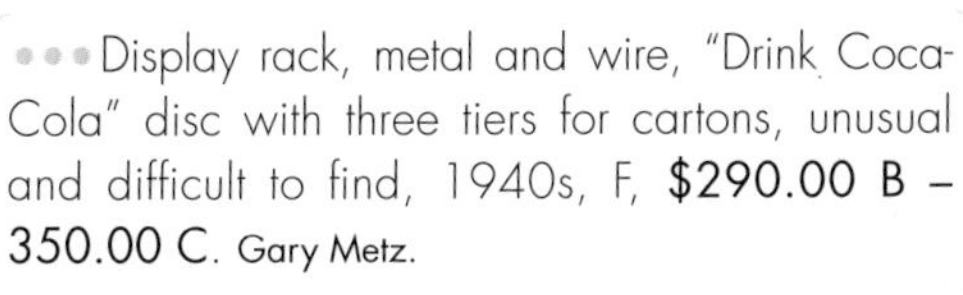

••• Display rack, metal and wire, "Drink Coca-Cola" disc with three tiers for cartons, unusual and difficult to find, 1940s, F, **$290.00 B – 350.00 C**. Gary Metz.

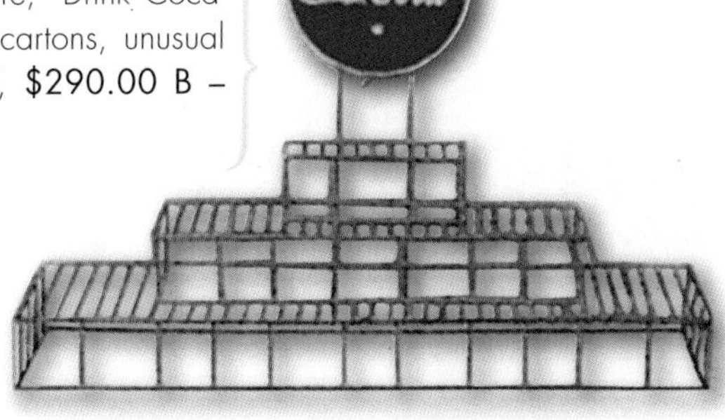

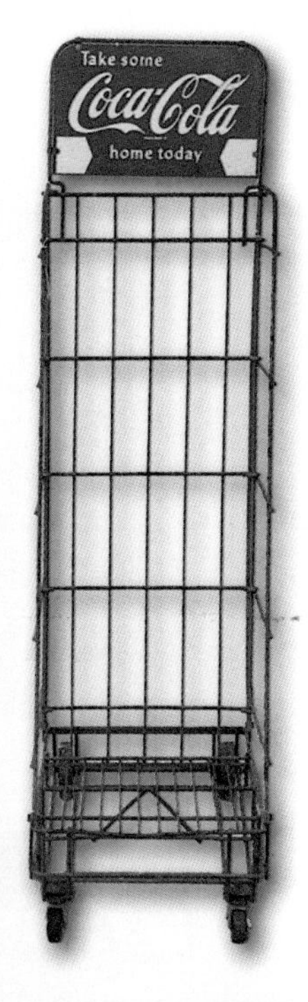

••• Display rack, metal and wire, "Take Some Coca-Cola Home Today," wire body with top courtesy panel and metal wheels on bottom, EX, **$295.00 – 350.00 C**.

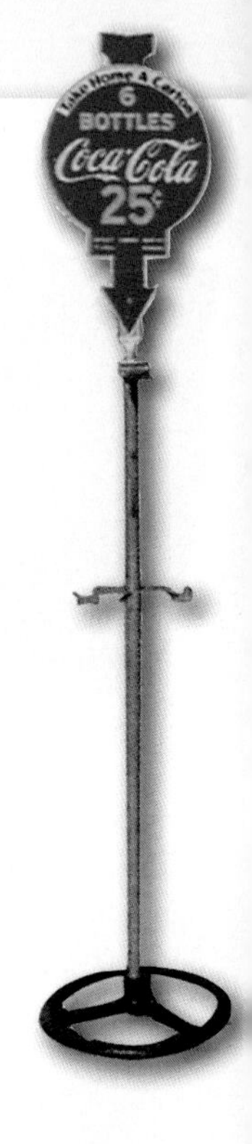

••• Display rack, metal, "Coca-Cola...6 Bottles 25¢," early and hard-to-find store fixture, 1930s, NM, $825.00 B. Gary Metz.

••• Display rack, metal, "Place Empties Here...Thank You," three-case store rack for placement beside a vending machine, G, $425.00 C.

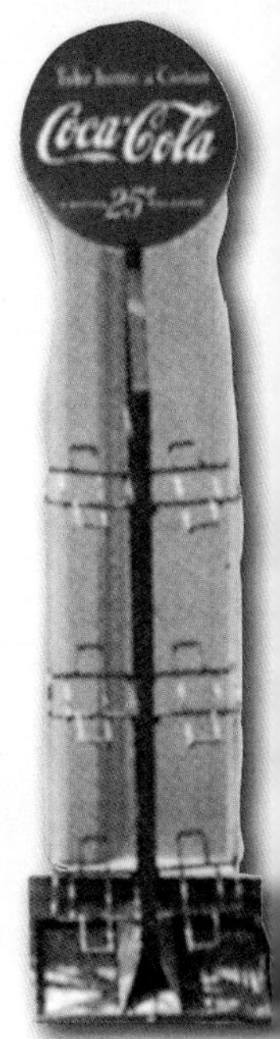

••• Display rack, metal, "Take Home a Carton...Coca-Cola," store carton display, round message panel at top, 1930s, 55" tall, VG, $500.00 B. Gary Metz.

••• Six-pack, aluminum, "Drink Coca-Cola" embossed and painted on sides, rolled wire handle with wooden grip, 1950s, EX, **$135.00 C**. Mitchell Collection.

••• Six-pack, aluminum, "Drink Coca-Cola... King Size," lettered on sides, wire handle, 1950s, EX, **$125.00 C**. Mitchell Collection.

••• Six-pack, cardboard, "Six bottles...Coca-Cola...Serve Ice Cold," with pull-up handle, 1930s, EX, **$145.00 C**. Mitchell Collection.

••• Six-pack, wood, "Pause...Go Refreshed," wire handle with wood grip and wood bottle compartments, wings under message on carton end, 1930s, EX, **$450.00 B**. Gary Metz.

••• Stadium vendor, metal, "Drink Coca-Cola," backpack with premix device and cup holder, white on red, 1950 – 1960s, G, **$525.00 B**. Gary Metz.

••• Stadium vendor, metal, "Drink Coca-Cola," with curved side toward vendor's body, insulated, with canvas carrying strap, original opener on end, 1940 – 1950s, VG, **$350.00 – 425.00 C**. Mitchell Collection.

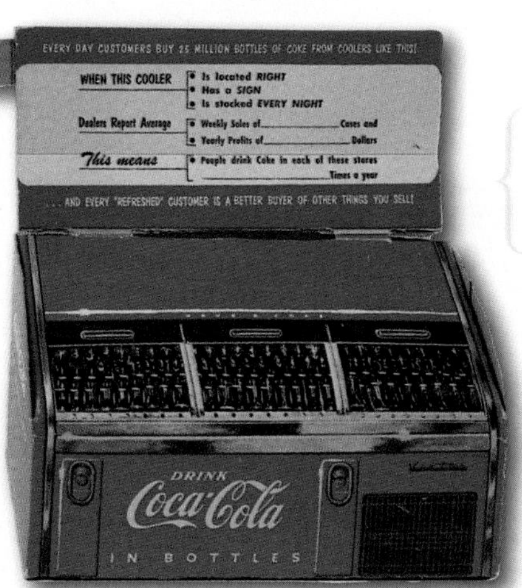

••• Chest, cardboard, "Drink Coca-Cola in Bottles," salesman's sample, 1940 – 1950s, G, **$195.00 C**. Mitchell Collection.

••• Chest, metal, "Drink Coca-Cola Ice Cold," lift-top bottle opener with cap catcher, will cool two cases, has no vending device, so it's an honor-system machine, 1940 – 1950s, 18½" x 18½" x 40¼", EX, $1,595.00 D – 2,000.00 C.

••• Chest, metal, "Drink Coca-Cola," salesman's sample of Westinghouse standard wet box with case storage under box, complete with opener and cap catcher, EX, **$2,400.00 C – 3,200.00 B**. Mitchell Collection.

••• Chest, wood and zinc, "Help Yourself...Drink Coca-Cola...Deposit in Box 5¢," very early lined box with side handles and hinged top, red on yellow, 1920s, VG, **$325.00 B**. Gary Metz.

••• Picnic, metal, "Drink Coca-Cola," Acton-produced unit still with original box, metal swing handle, tray is still inside, 1950 – 1960s, 17" x 12" x 19", EX, **$395.00 C**.

••• Picnic, metal, "Drink Coca-Cola," unusual round design with decal on outside and zinc liner inside, white on red, 1940s, 8" x 9", VG, **$250.00 B – 350.00 C**. Gary Metz.

••• Picnic, metal, "It's the Real Thing... Drink Coca-Cola," dynamic wave logo, wire handles on side with opening top, white on red, 1960s, 18" x 13" x 16½", G, **$185.00 D**. Patrick's Collectibles.

••• Picnic, stainless steel, "Drink Coca-Cola," airline cooler with top embossed "Northwest Airlines," unusual in the short body height, good top handle with snap-down locks, stainless steel, 1940 – 1950s, 9½" tall, EX, **$750.00 B – 895.00 C**. Gary Metz.

••• Store, metal and wood, "Serve Yourself...Drink Coca-Cola...Please Pay the Clerk," with original Starr opener and good zinc lining, 32" x 29" x 2¼", F, **$1,700.00 B**. Gary Metz.

••• Store, metal, "Drink Coca-Cola," Glascock junior complete with cap catcher, which is a hard-to-locate item, 1929, EX, **$2,200.00 – 3,000.00 C**. Mitchell Collection.

••• Store, metal, "Drink Coca-Cola," two-piece unit — top is picnic cooler and bottom is designed to sit on the floor and accept the top, 1950s, 17" x 12" x 39", EX, **$3,100.00 B**. Gary Metz.

••• Store, metal, "Serve Yourself... Drink Coca-Cola...Please Pay Cashier," salesman's sample Glascock, complete with miniature cases of bottles on storage rack beneath wet box, NM, **$2,300.00 – 3,300.00 C**. Mitchell Collection.

••• Store, wood and plastic, "Drink Coca-Cola," salesman's sample of counter dispenser, still with original carrying box, 1960s, 4½" x 6½" x 6¼", EX, **$2,500.00 B**. Gary Metz.

••• Store, wood and zinc, "Drink Coca-Cola Delicious Refreshing," wet box with zinc-lined inside, 1920s, 38" x 20" x 35", F, **$950.00 B**. Gary Metz.

••• Dispenser, metal, "No-Drip Protectors...Keeps Your Hands and Clothing Dry," self-serve dispenser, 1930s, 4½" x 8" x 2¼", EX, **$100.00 – 145.00 C**. Gary Metz.

••• Dispenser, metal, with two original sleeves and original box with mounting instructions, not marked, 6½" x 5", EX, **$170.00 B**. Autopia Advertising Auctions.

••• Paper, "Drink Coca-Cola...Delicious and Refreshing...A Great Drink...With Good Things to Eat," couple cooking outside and enjoying a bottle of Coke, 1930 – 1940s, 3¾" x 6½", EX, **$14.00 – 20.00 C.** B. J. Summers.

••• Paper, "Drink Coca-Cola...Delicious and Refreshing...The Drink Everybody Knows," with different version of the bottle in hand, 1930 – 1940s, 3¾" x 6½", EX, **$10.00 – 14.00 C.** B. J. Summers.

••• Paper, "It's the Real Thing," pretty lady with bottle of Coke, 1920 – 1930s, 3¾" x 6½", EX, **$8.00 – 12.00 C.** B. J. Summers.

●●● Changer, metal, "Drink Coca-Cola... Serve Yourself," made by Vendo Co., with 1938 and 1940 dates, 8" x 8½" x 4½", VG, **$150.00 – 200.00 C**.

●●● Chest, metal, "Coca-Cola," decal lettering, lift-top lid, bottle opener and cap catcher, 32" x 18" x 41", F, **$700.00 D**.

●●● Chest, metal, "Drink Coca-Cola," Cavalier C-27 with lift top and star handle, sought after in part because of the size, white on red, 1940 – 1950, 18" x 22" x 41", EX, **$1,400.00 B**. Gary Metz.

●●● Chest, metal, "Drink Coca-Cola...Ice Cold," Westinghouse 10-case master, top lid hinges in the middle and lifts from both ends, 1950s, 30½" x 36" x 45", NM, **$1,850.00 D**. Patrick's Collectibles.

●●● Chest, metal, "Drink Coca-Cola in Bottles... Ice Cold," Vendo #23, also known as the spin top, found in standard and deluxe models (depends on top and other colors), 1950s, 24" x 36" x 21", EX, **$1,395.00 – 1,695.00 D**.

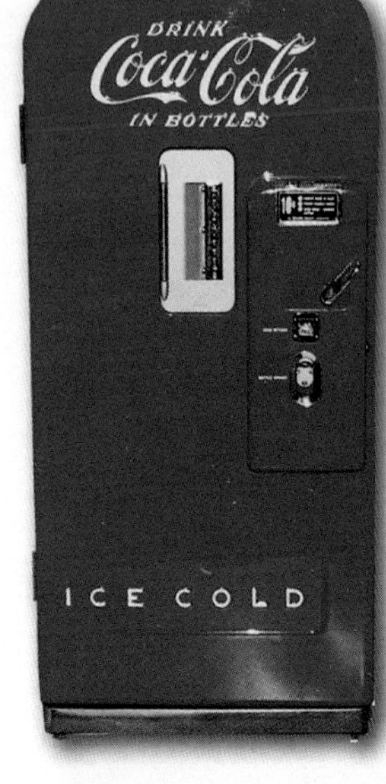

••• Upright, metal, "Drink Coca-Cola in Bottles," Vendo V-39, very desirable machine due to its small size, also fairly common and easy to find, 1940 – 1950s, 27" x 58" x 16", NM, **$2,995.00 D – 3,100.00 C**. Patrick's Collectibles.

••• Upright, metal, "Drink Coca-Cola in Bottles," Vendo V-81, a much sought-after machine for home use mostly due to its size and eye appeal, 1950s, 27" x 58" x 16", VG, **$1,500.00 – 2,000.00 C**. Mike and Debbie Summers.

••• Upright, metal, Vendo #44, "Drink Coca-Cola," two tone with white top and red bottom, 1950s, 16" x 57½" x 15½", NM, **$2,400.00 B – 2,750.00 C**. Gary Metz.

Radios

••• Bottle, Bakelite, "Drink Coca-Cola," shaped like a hobbleskirt bottle, made by Crosley, Cincinnati, 1930s (1931 – 1934), 7½" dia. x 24" tall, EX, **\$5,500.00 B**. Gary Metz.

••• Can, plastic, "Enjoy Coca-Cola" and dynamic wave, 1970s, EX, **\$50.00 C**. Mitchell Collection.

••• Cooler, plastic and metal, "Coca-Cola Refreshes You Best," an extremely hard-to-locate item, designed to resemble an airline cooler, top lifts to reveal controls, 1950s, G, **\$3,800.00 B**. Gary Metz.

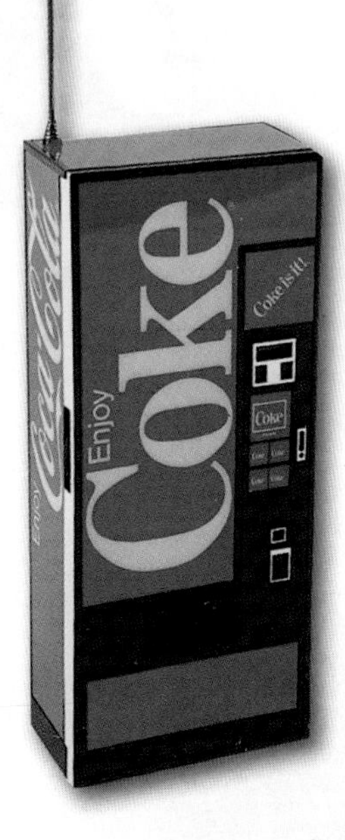

●●● Vending machine, plastic, "Coke," upright machine, 1980s, EX, **$95.00 C**. Mitchell Collection.

●●● Vending machine, plastic, "Drink Coca-Cola," upright machine with double drop chute, F, **$200.00 C**. Mitchell Collection.

●●● Vending machine, plastic, "Enjoy Coke," upright design with vertical dynamic wave panel and push button selectors on right, 1970s, EX, **$135.00 C**. Mitchell Collection.

Clocks

Anniversary, glass and metal, "Drink Coca-Cola" in center of clock face, small miniature bottles on bottom movements, covered by clear glass dome, 1950s, 3" x 5", EX, **$975.00 – 1,100.00 C**. Mitchell Collection.

Boudoir, leather, "Drink Bottled Coca-Cola...So Easily Served," shaped like a straight-sided bottle, gold lettering, 1910, 3" x 8", VG, **$1,500.00 B – 2,000.00 C**. Gary Metz.

Counter, metal and glass, "Drink Coca-Cola...Serve Yourself," light-up with clock to left of message panel, 1950s, 20" x 9", EX, **$925.00 – 1,400.00 C**. Note: There were several versions of this clock produced. All are very desirable.

••• Counter, metal and glass, "Pause... Drink Coca-Cola" with Art Deco influence and great crinkle paint, large round clock at top, "Drink Coca-Cola" message panel below, rare piece, 1930s, EX, **$5,700.00 C**. Mitchell Collection.

••• Desk, celluloid, "Drink Coca-Cola...," featuring Hilda Clark and round clock dial at lower left, 1901, 5½" x 7¼", EX, **$9,000.00 C**.

••• Desk, leather, "Drink Coca-Cola in Bottles," with gold lettering and gold hobbleskirt bottle at lower left and right, rare item, 1910, 4⅓" x 6", EX, **$1,400.00 C**.

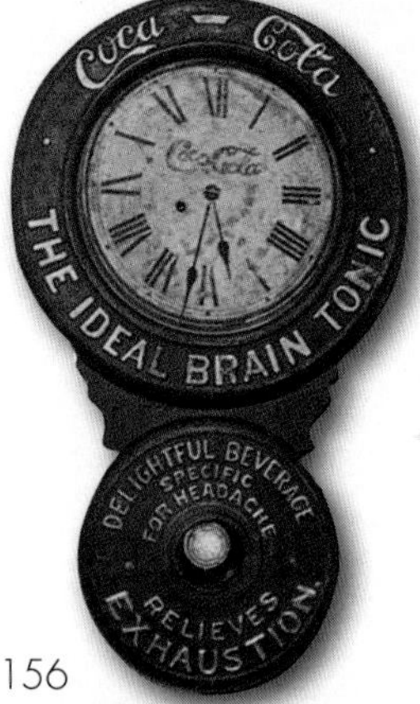

••• Wall, composition, "Coca-Cola...the Ideal Brain Tonic," Baird Clock Co., 1891 – 1895, 24" tall, EX, **$5,300.00 D – 9,700.00 B**.

••• Wall, metal and glass, "Drink Coca-Cola," in center red dot, 14½" dia., EX, **$575.00 C**.

••• Wall, metal and glass, "Drink Coca-Cola," with center fishtail logo, green background, NOS, 1960s, EX, **$325.00 C**.

••• Wall, metal and glass, "Drink Coca-Cola," with silhouette girl in spotlight at bottom, 1930 – 1940s, 18" dia., VG, **$775.00 B**. Gary Metz.

••• Wall, metal and glass, neon, "Drink Coca-Cola" in center with spotlight bottle at bottom, green wrinkle paint on outside, 1930s, 16" x 16", EX, **$825.00 B – 1,000.00 C**. Gary Metz.

••• Wall, metal and glass, neon, "Ice Cold Coca-Cola," with spotlight silhouette girl at bottom of circle, 1940s, 18" x 18", VG, **$1,600.00 B**. Gary Metz.

••• Wall, metal and wood, "Coca-Cola," round red dot Telechron clock with wings, 36", VG, **$500.00 C**. Mitchell Collection.

••• Wall, wood and glass, "In Bottles," Gilbert regulator that hung in many bottlers' offices. This one hung in the old location of the Paducah Coca-Cola Bottling Co. office on Jackson St. This clock has only had three owners since the early removal from the Coke office. 1920 – 1930s, EX, **$2,100.00 – 2,400.00 C**. Mitchell Collection.

••• Wall, wood, "Drink Coca-Cola," Welch octagon schoolhouse, 1901, EX, **$1,800.00 D**.

••• Wall, wood, glass, and composition, "Drink Coca-Cola 5¢ Delicious Refreshing," Baird Clock Co., 15-day movement, 1896 – 1899, EX, **$6,725.00 C**.

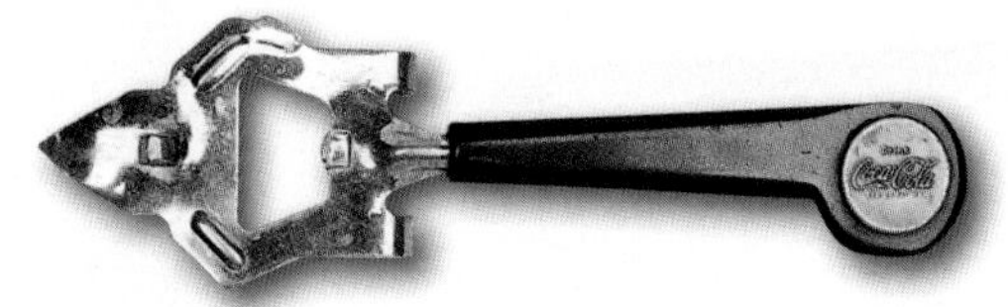

••• Handheld, metal and Bakelite, bottle opener and can opener combination, 1950s, EX, **$65.00 D**.

••• Handheld, metal, "Coca-Cola Bottles," key style with Prest-o-lite square hold in end, EX, **$55.00 D**.

••• Handheld, metal, "Drink Bottled Coca-Cola," saber shaped, 1920s, EX, **$200.00 D**.

••• Handheld, metal, "Drink Coca-Cola in Bottles," brass, key design with the Prest-o-lite valve hole, 1910s, EX, **$125.00 D**. Mitchell Collection.

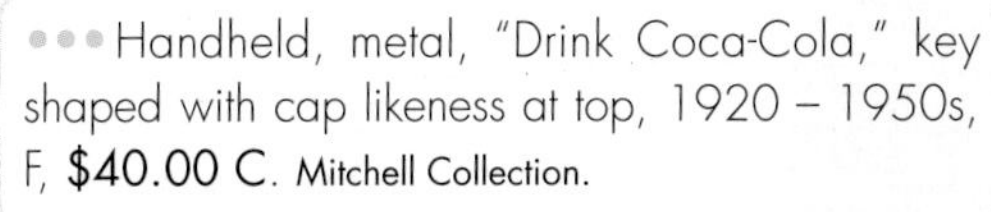

••• Handheld, metal, "Drink Coca-Cola," key shaped with cap likeness at top, 1920 – 1950s, F, **$40.00 C**. Mitchell Collection.

••• Handheld, metal, "Drink Coca-Cola," straight, 1910 – 1950s, EX, **$35.00 – 40.00 C**. Mitchell Collection.

••• Handheld, metal, "Have a Coke," beer-type opener, EX, **$8.00 C**. Mitchell Collection.

••• Wall mount, corkscrew, 1920s, EX, **$85.00 C**. Mitchell Collection.

••• Wall mount, "Drink Coca-Cola," with original box, "The Starr 'X' manufactured...by Brown Manufacturing Co.," 1940 – 1980s, EX, **$35.00 D**. Mitchell Collection.

••• Wall mount, metal, "Drink Coca-Cola," known as bent metal opener, 1950s, EX, **$25.00 C**. Mitchell Collection.

"Coca-Cola Bottling Company," one blade and opener, 1910s, EX, **$350.00 C**. Mitchell Collection.

"The Coca-Cola Bottling Co.…Kaster and Co., Germany," blade and corkscrew (many reproductions), 1905 – 1915, EX, **$450.00 C**. Mitchell Collection.

"Drink Coca-Cola," two blades, G, **$45.00 C**. Mitchell Collection.

Ice Picks

Bulb handle, wood and metal, "Coca-Cola" painted in black on handle, 1920s, VG, **$65.00 C**. Mitchell Collection.

Round handle, wood and metal, bottle opener on end of handle, "Drink Coca-Cola in Bottles" in black on handle, 1920 – 1930s, EX, **$50.00 C**. Mitchell Collection.

Square handle, wood and metal, "Coca-Cola in Bottles...Ice-Coal...Phone 87," in painted black lettering on handle, 1930 – 1940s, EX, **$35.00 C**. Mitchell Collection.

Ashtrays

••• Desk, ceramic, "Partners...Coca-Cola" with facsmile of baseball in circle, 1950s, 7¼" sq., EX, **$85.00 B**. Gary Metz.

••• Tabletop, Bakelite and metal, match pull from top of bottle, easily the most sought after of all Coke ashtrays, 1940s, EX, **$1,500.00 – 2,100.00 C**. Expect to pay $300.00 – 600.00 for the match refills for this ashtray. Mitchell Collection.

••• Tabletop, ceramic and plastic, "Drink Coca-Cola" logo in bowl, miniature bottle on edge, from Canadian bottler, 1950s, EX, **$250.00 B**. Gary Metz.

Ashtrays

••• Tabletop, glass, "Coca-Cola Bottling Company...Dickson, Tennessee, Coca-Cola...Jerry Humphreys," with four cigarette groves, EX, **$25.00 C**. Mitchell Collection.

••• Tabletop, metal and plastic, bottle lighter in center with six cigarette grooves, 1950s, EX, **$300.00 – 350.00 C**. Mitchell Collection.

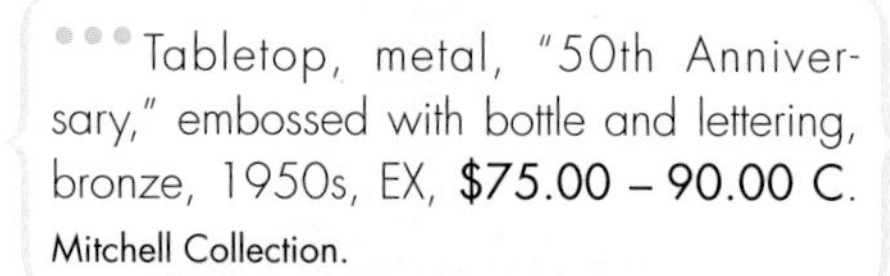

••• Tabletop, metal, "50th Anniversary," embossed with bottle and lettering, bronze, 1950s, EX, **$75.00 – 90.00 C**. Mitchell Collection.

••• Tabletop, metal, "Enjoy Coca-Cola," molded cigarette holders and lettering with dynamic wave logo, EX, **$35.00 – 40.00 C**. Mitchell Collection.

••• Pocket, metal, "Drink Coca-Cola," 1950s, EX, **$35.00 – 45.00 C**. Mitchell Collection.

••• Pocket, metal, "Drink Coca-Cola," musical when lit, 1970s, EX, **$225.00 – 250.00 C**. Mitchell Collection.

••• Tabletop, Bakelite, pen holder and miniature bottle, 1950s, EX, **$195.00 – 255.00 C**. Mitchell Collection.

••• Tabletop, metal, "Coke," can shaped with dynamic wave contour, 1960 – 1970s, M, **$45.00 – 55.00 C**. Mitchell Collection.

●●● Holder, tabletop, metal, "Drink Coca-Cola...Be Really Refreshed!" Books could be pulled out from the bottom and refilled from the top. 1959, EX, **$195.00 – 245.00 C**. Mitchell Collection.

●●● Matchbook, "A Distinctive Drink in a Distinctive Bottle," 1922, EX, **$125.00 – 140.00 C**. Mitchell Collection.

●●● Matchbook, "Drink Coca-Cola," mock-up of Westinghouse vending machine, EX, **$90.00 – 115.00 C**.

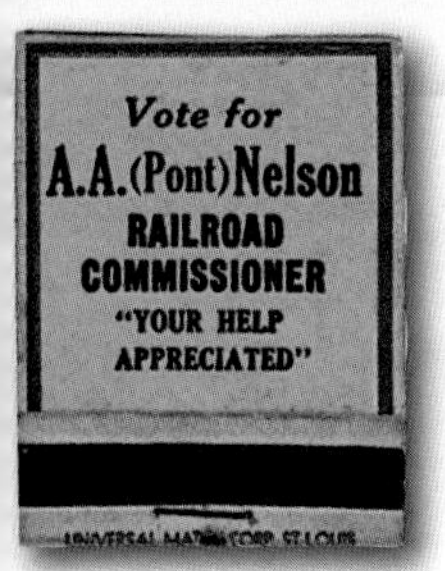

Matchbook, "Vote for A.A. (Pont) Nelson, Railroad Commissioner," VG, **$8.00 – 12.00 C**. Mitchell Collection.

Match safe, pocket, porcelain, "Compliments of Coca-Cola Bottling Co....Union City, Tenn.," combination safe and striker, 1930s, EX, **$300.00 – 400.00 C**. Mitchell Collection.

Wall hung, metal, "Drink Coca-Cola in Bottles...Coca-Cola Bottling Co.," 1940s, fair, **$375.00 – 435.00 C**. Mitchell Collection.

Wall hung, porcelain, "Drink Coca-Cola... Strike Matches Here," 1939, NM, **$400.00 B – 450.00 C**. Gary Metz.

••• Paper, "Drink Coca-Cola" on one side and advertising for the 37th American Legion Convention in Miami, Florida, Oct. 10 – 13, 1955, on the other. VG, **$40.00 – 45.00 C**.

••• Paper, "Please Put Empties in the Rack," bottle being placed in bottle rack, EX, **$10. 00 – 12.00 C**.

••• Paper, "Things Go Better with Coke" in square outline inside of circle, EX, **$10.00 – 12.00 C**.

••• Paper, "Things Go Better with Coke," scalloped edges, mint, **$8.00 – 12.00 C**. Mitchell Collection.

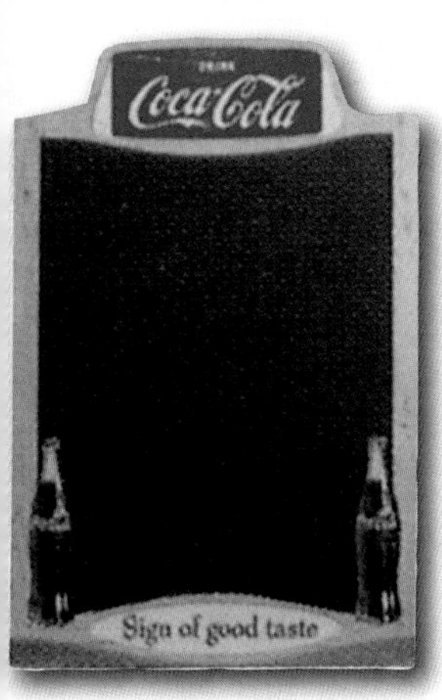

••• Wall hung, cardboard, "Drink Coca-Cola…Sign of Good Taste," bottle on each side of message panel, 1959, 19" x 28", NM, **$250.00 B**. Gary Metz.

••• Wall hung, cardboard, "Have a Coke," button at top and double bottles at bottom, 1940s, VG, **$225.00 – 255.00 C**.

••• Wall hung, metal, "Drink Coca-Cola," bottle with tag-type panel at top of message area, chalkboard design, EX, **$200.00 – 275.00 D**. Riverside Antique Mall.

HOT DOGS.............. 10¢
ICE CREAM OR PIE........... 15¢
HAMBURGER PLATE.......... 47¢
SPAGHETTI & MEATBALLS ...... 60¢
COCA COLA & SODAS .... 5¢
DRINK
Coca-Cola
IN BOTTLES
CHILI CON CARNE......... 15¢
TUNA FISH SANDWICH....... 29¢
ROAST BEEF SANDWICH........ 55¢
MALTS & SHAKES .... 15¢
FRENCH FRIES .... 10¢

••• Wall hung, metal, "Drink Coca-Cola in Bottles," button in center, 1950s, 60" x 14", NM, **$2,300.00 B**. Gary Metz.

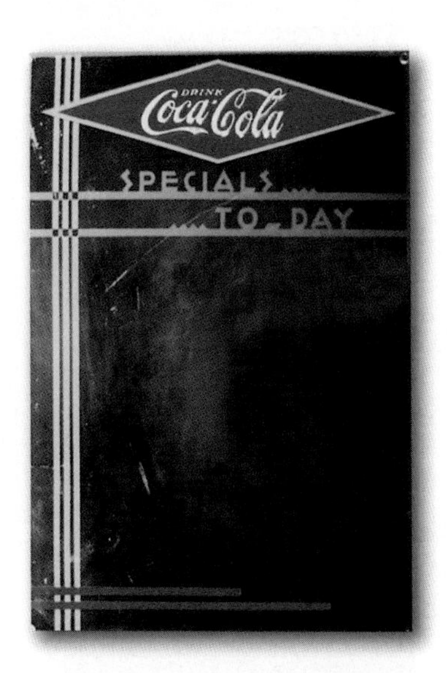

••• Wall hung, metal, "Drink Coca-Cola... Specials To-day," diamond logo at top, chalkboard design, 1931, EX, **$300.00 – 450.00 D**. Riverside Antique Mall.

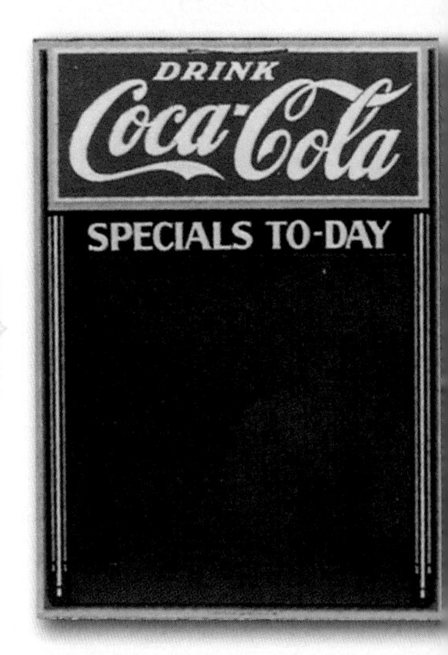

••• Wall hung, metal, "Drink Coca-Cola...Specials To-day," product panel at top, chalkboard design, Canadian, difficult to locate, 1938, 17" x 24", NM, **$650.00 B**. Gary Metz.

Menu Boards

••• Wall hung, wood and metal, "Drink Coca-Cola," button at bottom, slide menu strips, 1940s, EX, **$650.00 B – 725.00 C**. Gary Metz.

••• Wall hung, wood and metal, "Drink Coca-Cola in Bottles," slide-type menu slots with 16" dia. button at top, Kay Displays, 17" x 29", EX, **$525.00 B – 675.00 C**. Gary Metz.

••• Wall hung, wood and metal, "Drink Coca-Cola," panel at bottom, slide-type menu strips, 1940s, EX, **$675.00 – 800.00 C**. Mitchell Collection.

••• Bar, metal, "Drink Coca-Cola delicious refreshing," silhouette girl in yellow spotlight on left side of bar, 1939, 28" x 3½", NM, **$500.00 B**. Gary Metz.

••• Bar, porcelain, "Drink Coca-Cola...Ice Cold...in Bottles," 1940 – 1950s, 30" wide, M, **$1,000.00 B**. Gary Metz.

••• Bar, porcelain, "Ice Cold Coca-Cola in Bottles," reverse side has "Thank You, Call Again," 1930s, 25" x 3¼" NM, **$475.00 B**. Gary Metz.

••• Bar, porcelain, "Refreshing Coca-Cola New Feeling," 1950 – 1960s, EX, **$195.00 – 235.00 C**. Mitchell Collection.

Door Pushes

••• Flat plate, porcelain, "Pull... Refresh Yourself...Drink Coca-Cola," matching "Push...," 1950s, 4" x 8", EX, **$450.00 – 725.00 D**.

••• Handle, aluminum, "Drink Coca-Cola," in shape of bottle, 1930s, NM, **$275.00 – 300.00 D**. Charlie's Antique Mall.

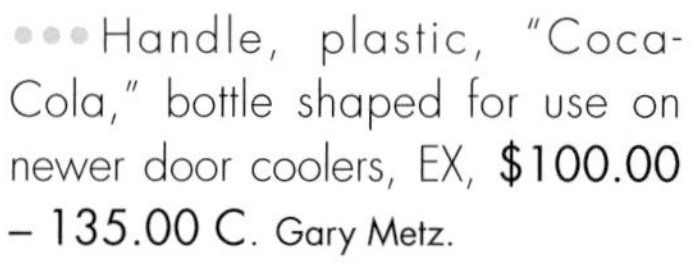

••• Handle, plastic, "Coca-Cola," bottle shaped for use on newer door coolers, EX, **$100.00 – 135.00 C**. Gary Metz.

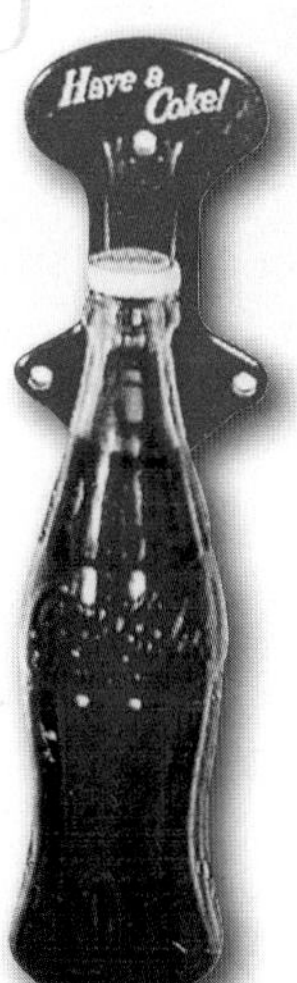

••• Handle, plastic, Coca-Cola bottle-shaped screen door pull, "Have a Coke" mounting bracket, 8" long, EX, **$150.00 C**. Buffalo Bay Auction Co.

••• Buddy L #5546, metal, "Enjoy Coca-Cola the Pause That Refreshes!" complete with original box and all accessories, yellow, 1956, NM, **$725.00 B**. Gary Metz.

••• Buddy L #5646, metal, "Drink Coca-Cola the Pause That Refreshes!" with original box, yellow GMC, 1957, EX, **$675.00 B**. Gary Metz.

••• Buddy L, metal, "Drink Coca-Coca the Pause That Refreshes!" with original miniature cases and bottles, 1960s, EX, **$325.00 – 450.00 C**.

••• German #426-20, metal, rubber, and plastic, "Drink Coca-Cola," wind-up with fantastic detailing and a load of cases and bottles, 1949, EX, **$2,600.00 B**. Gary Metz.

••• Marx, metal, "Drink Coca-Cola Delicious Refreshing," side load, with wheel skirts on both back and front fender wells, 1950s, G, **$250.00 – 325.00 C**. Gary Metz.

••• Marx, metal, "Drink Coca-Cola Delicious Refreshing," snub-nose cab with full load of cases and bottles, 1950s, VG, **$450.00 – 500.00 C**.

••• Marx, plastic, "Drink Coca-Cola Delicious Refreshing," Ford style with side load full of cases and bottles, 1950s, EX, **$375.00 B**. Gary Metz.

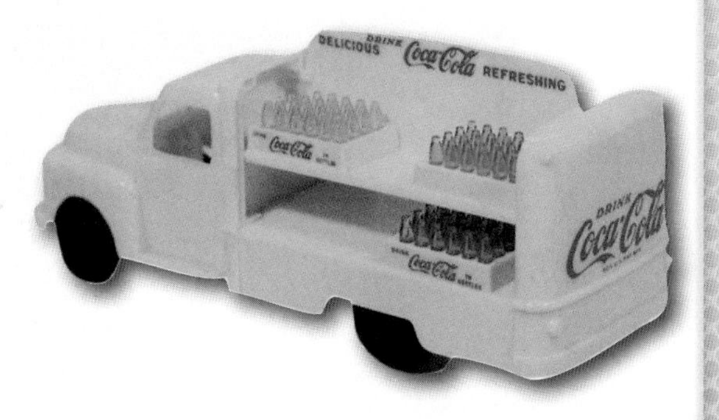

••• Marx, plastic, "Drink Coca-Cola Iced," in original box with double cases on sides and wooden wheels, Canadian, 1950s, EX, **$1,400.00 C**.

••• Metalcraft, metal, "Coca-Cola... Every Bottle Sterlized," rubber tires, with glass bottles on loading bed, 1930s, G, **$775.00 C**. Mitchell Collection.

••• Sanyo, metal, "Drink Coca-Cola," made in Japan and distributed by Allen Haddock Company in Atlanta, Georgia, working head- and taillights, still with original box, 1950 – 1960s, EX, **$325.00 B – 395.00 C**. Gary Metz.

••• Tractor trailer, metal, "Drink Coca-Cola...," red with spotlight carton on trailer, still in box, but the box is less than EX, **$225.00 – 245.00 C**.

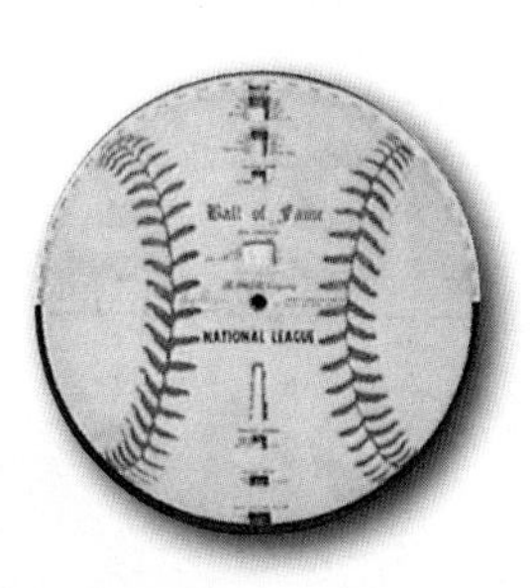

••• Baseball hall of fame information, cardboard, Coca-Cola premium, information about the Hall of Fame for both the National and American Leagues, 1901 – 1960, EX, **$95.00 B – 150.00 D**. Gary Metz.

••• Buddy Lee, composition, "Drink Coca-Cola" patches on doll uniform that stills has the original tag, 1950s, 12" tall, EX, **$875.00 B**. Gary Metz.

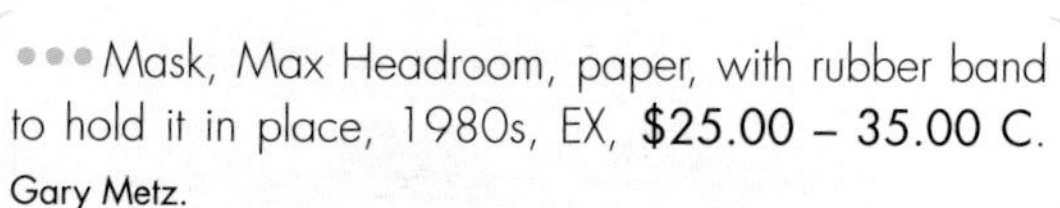

••• Mask, Max Headroom, paper, with rubber band to hold it in place, 1980s, EX, **$25.00 – 35.00 C**. Gary Metz.

••• Roller skates, metal and leather, "Drink Coca-Cola in Bottles...Pat. Aug 16, 1914," thought to be from the St. Louis Bottling Company, 1914, VG, **$900.00 B**. Gary Metz.

••• Shopping basket, metal and cardboard, child's size with products printed on sides, a six-pack of Coca-Cola in plain view and small boxes of products inside basket, 1950s, EX, **$450.00 C – 600.00 D**. Mitchell Collection.

••• Train, Express Limited, plastic and metal, Coke train with advertising on each car, in original box with all accessories present, 1960s, EX, **$450.00 C – 525.00 D**.

•••Building, plastic, "You'll Feel Right at Home Drinking Coca-Cola," EX, **$135.00 – 165.00 C**.

•••Can, metal, "Bevete Coca-Cola," dynamic wave logo for the foreign market, top money drop, EX, **$95.00 – 115.00 C**.

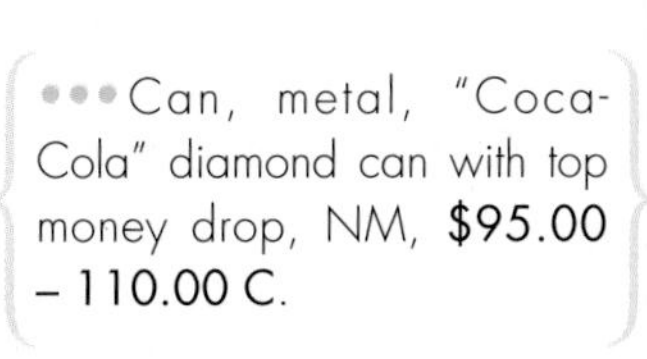

•••Can, metal, "Coca-Cola" diamond can with top money drop, NM, **$95.00 – 110.00 C**.

ADVERTISING DEPT
Coca-Cola
1/43 1950 DELIVERY TRUCK BANK
1/43 TIRELIRE EN FORME DE 1950 CAMIONNETTE

••• Truck, metal, "Coca-Cola...Advertising Dept.," in original box with top coin drop on bed of truck, NM, **$35.00 – 65.00 C**. Gary Metz.

••• Truck, metal, "Drink Coca-Cola...Coca-Cola Bottling Co.," panel design with money drop on top, in original box, NM, **$45.00 – 75.00 C**. Gary Metz.

••• Truck, plastic and metal, "Coca-Cola," delivery van with dynamic wave on side, top money drop, EX, **$45.00 – 75.00 C**.

••• Vending machine, plastic, "Drink Coca-Cola... Play Refreshed," 1950s, EX, **$145.00 – 195.00 C**. Mitchell Collection.

••• Cards, plastic, "Drink Coca-Cola," lady with dog, unopened package, 1943, M, **$235.00 – 250.00 C**.

••• Cards, plastic, "Drink Coca-Cola," military nurse in uniform with a bottle of Coke, 1943, M, **$145.00 – 185.00 C**. Mitchell Collection.

••• Cards, plastic, "Drink Coca-Cola," wartime spotter lady, 1943, M, **$125.00 – 145.00 C**. Mitchell Collection.

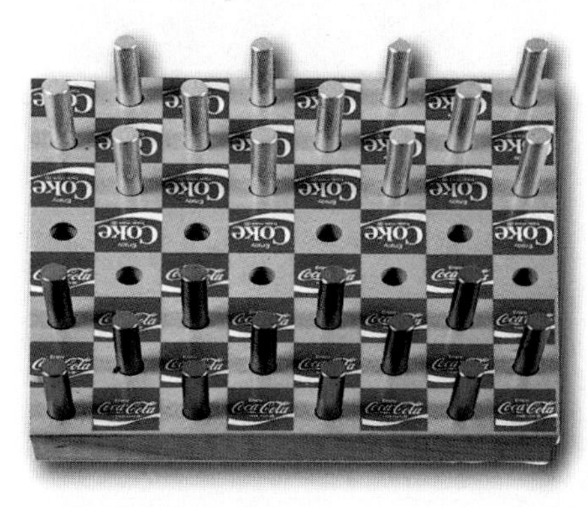

••• Checkers, wood and metal, "Coca-Cola" with dynamic wave logo on board, modern version with metal pegs for the actual checker pieces, 1970s, EX, **$65.00 – 85.00 C**. Mitchell Collection.

••• Checkers, wood, "Coca-Cola" in script on top of each checker, in original cardboard box that is marked "Compliments of the Coca-Cola Bottling Company," 1940 – 1950s, EX, **$45.00 – 75.00 C**. Mitchell Collection.

•••Flip game, cardboard, "Drink Coca-Cola in Sterlized Bottles," framed and under glass, 1910 – 1920, VG, **$875.00 – 1,000.00 C**. Mitchell Collection.

••• Puzzle, cardboard, "Coke Adds Life to Everything Nice," potpourri puzzle with over 2,000 pieces in original unopened box, EX, **$55.00 – 65.00 C**. Mitchell Collection.

••• Puzzle, cardboard, "Drink Coca-Cola Ice Cold," 1,000 pieces in original box with scene of young lovers on a Coke cooler in front of an old country store, EX, **$25.00 – 45.00 C**. Gary Metz.

••• Badge, enamel and gold with diamonds, "100,000" gallon award, given to Wilmington, North Carolina, bottler George Hutaff, rare item, 1935, EX, $4,500.00 B – 10,000.00 C. Gary Metz.

••• Case, metal, Coca-Cola bottle in raised center top position, snap-front closure, EX, $75.00 – 100.00 C. Mitchell Collection.

••• Cuff links, metal, "Enjoy Coca-Cola" on glass-shaped links, gold finish, 1970s, EX, $65.00 – 85.00 C. Mitchell Collection.

Earrings, metal, Coca-Cola bottles, for pierced ears, still on original card, dynamic wave logo, NM, $20.00 – 25.00 C.

Money clip, metal, "Compliments Coca-Cola Bottling Works, Nashville, Tennessee," EX, $95.00 – 100.00 C. Mitchell Collection.

Tie tac, metal, "Coca-Cola," employee recognition for 30 years of service, with original box, NM, $45.00 – 60.00 C. Mitchell Collection.

••• Apron, cloth, "Be Really Refreshed! Drink Coca-Cola," full front with two pockets, 1959 – 1960s, VG, **$35.00 – 55.00 C**. Mitchell Collection.

••• Bandana, cloth, "Kit Carson" and "Drink Coca-Cola," red with Kit in center and western scenes, plus Coke logos in each corner, 1950s, 20" x 22", EX, **$75.00 – 125.00 C**. Mitchell Collection.

••• Belt, web, "Enjoy Coca-Cola" on metal buckle with dynamic wave logo, 1960s, NM, **$20.00 – 30.00 C**.

••• Belt, web, "Enjoy Coca-Cola" on metal buckle with white and red dynamic wave logo, EX, **$20.00 – 30.00 C**.

••• Coat, cloth, "Enjoy Coca-Cola... Central States Bottling Co.," green waist-length driver's jacket with zip-in quilted lining for light or heavy weather use, EX, **$45.00 – 65.00 C**.

••• Coat, cloth, "Enjoy Coca-Cola," dynamic wave logo on front. This driver's uniform was known as the "hunting jacket" due to the large pockets, the length, and the duck material. Riverside manufacturer's tag still in place, unused, brown, EX, **$55.00 – 75.00 C**. Gary Metz.

••• Hat, cloth, "Drink Coca-Cola... Delicious and Refreshing," felt beanie with red, white, and green panels, 1930 – 1940s, 8" dia., VG, **$55.00 – 95.00 C**. Mitchell Collection.

••• Hat, cloth, "Drink Coca-Cola," driver's hat with round patch at crown and hard bill, becoming very difficult to locate, EX, **$140.00 – 200.00 C**.

••• Hat, cloth, "Drink Coca-Cola," round logo on side of folding soda fountain attendant that, NM, **$55.00 B – 125.00 C**. Autopia Advertising Auctions.

••• Hat, cloth, "Enjoy Coca-Cola" on crown of cowboy hat, employee award item still in original hat, never worn, NM, **$150.00 – 185.00 C**.

••• Patch, cloth, "Enjoy Coca-Cola," round jacket patch, 1950 – 1960s, EX, **$20.00 – 40.00 C**. Mitchell Collection.

••• Shirt, cloth, "Drink Coca-Cola," round patch on back of driver's shirt with "Things Go Better..." patch on one sleeve and hard-to-find "Fresca" sleeve patch on the other arm, 1960s, VG, **$60.00 – 85.00 C**. Mitchell Collection.

••• Shirt, cloth, "Drink Coca-Cola," round patch on back of striped driver's shirt, VG, **$45.00 – 55.00 C**. Mitchell Collection.

Shirt, cloth, "Things Go Better with Coke," bowler's shirt with lettering on back, 1960s, EX, **$30.00 – 45.00 C**. Mitchell Collection.

Tie, cloth, "Enjoy Coca-Cola," with dynamic wave in red box on brown background, EX, **$15.00 – 20.00 C**.

Uniform pants and shirt, cloth, "Enjoy Coca-Cola," driver's issue by Riverside, still in original packaging, dynamic wave cloth patch, NM, **$65.00 – 95.00 C**.

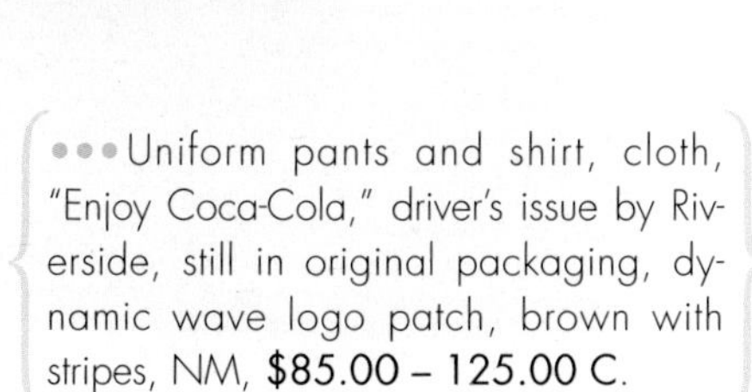

Uniform pants and shirt, cloth, "Enjoy Coca-Cola," driver's issue by Riverside, still in original packaging, dynamic wave logo patch, brown with stripes, NM, **$85.00 – 125.00 C**.

••• Uniform pants and shirt, "Enjoy Coca-Cola," driver's set with dynamic wave cloth patch, white shirt with green pants, EX, **$55.00 – 75.00 C**.

••• Vest, cloth, "Enjoy Coca-Cola" cloth patch on chest, green, issued to drivers, EX, **$35.00 – 55.00 C**.

••• Vest, cloth, "Enjoy Coca-Cola," insulated uniform item with dynamic wave cloth patch over front pocket, this style seems to be the most popular with collectors, red, EX, **$45.00 – 55.00 C**.

••• Bi-fold, leather, "When Thirsty Try a Bottle," gold engraving, ribbed texture, 1920s, EX, **$100.00 – 130.00 C**.

••• Coin purse, "Compliments of the Coca-Cola Bottling Co., Memphis, Tenn.," metal and celluloid top and snap, 1910 – 1920s, VG, **$195.00 – 225.00 C**. Mitchell Collection.

••• Coin purse, leather, "When Thirsty Try a Bottle," 1907, EX, **$100.00 – 125.00 C**. Mitchell Collection.

••• Tri-fold, plastic, "Enjoy Coca-Cola" in gold lettering, 1960s, EX, **$15.00 – 20.00 C**. Mitchell Collection.

••• Ad, paper, "And the Same to You," Santa in armchair with bottle of Coke, *National Geographic,* 1939, 7" x 10", VG, **$8.00 – 12.00 C.** B. J. Summers.

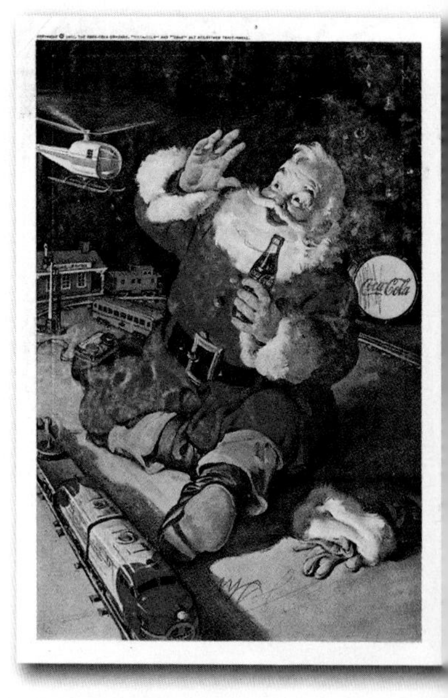

••• Ad, paper, "Coca-Cola," Santa with Coke bottle in the middle of train setup and with helicopter, 1962, 7" x 10", VG, **$8.00 – 10.00 C.** B. J. Summers.

••• Ad, paper, "Give and Take Say I," Santa with a Coke and a turkey leg, with black and white inset promoting cold Cokes "from your own refrigerator," 1937, 7" x 10", VG, **$8.00 – 10.00 C.** B. J. Summers.

••• Ad, paper, "The Pause That Refreshes...Coca-Cola," Santa in easy chair and surrounded by elves, 1960, 7" x 10", VG, **$8.00 – 10.00 C.** B. J. Summers.

••• Bottle hanger, paper, "'Twas the Night Before Christmas," Santa at refrigerator, 1950s, EX, **$50.00 – 65.00 C.** Mitchell Collection.

••• Calendar, paper, "Me, Too!" full monthly sheets, former owner had recorded the temperatures on each day, 1954, VG, **$150.00 B – 195.00 C**. Gary Metz.

••• Calendar, paper, "Presented by your Coca-Cola Bottler," with helicopter flying around Santa who is holding a bottle, reference edition, 1963, M, **$50.00 – 75.00 C**. Mitchell Collection.

••• Carton stuffer, cardboard, "Good Taste for All," Santa with a bottle of Coke, EX, **$75.00 – 85.00 C**. Mitchell Collection.

••• Display, cardboard, "Coca-Cola," die-cut easel back that folds out to 3-D effect with little boy in pj's surprising Santa, 1950s, VG, **$250.00 – 300.00 C**. Mitchell Collection.

••• Display, cardboard, "Coca-Cola," die-cut Santa on a stool holding a small wooden rabbit, EX, **$125.00 – 150.00 C**. Mitchell Collection.

••• Display, cardboard, "Greetings for Coca-Cola," die-cut standup with a Coke, 1948, 5' tall, F, **$265.00 – 275.00 C**. Mitchell Collection.

••• Display, cardboard, "Greetings from Coca-Cola," die-cut Santa with elbow on newel post enjoying a bottle of Coke, 1946, 6" x 12", EX, **$225.00 – 245.00 C.** Mitchell Collection.

••• Display, cardboard, "The Gift for Thirst," die-cut easel back with Santa in front of gifts, 1953, 9" x 18", EX, **$230.00 – 250.00 C.** Mitchell Collection.

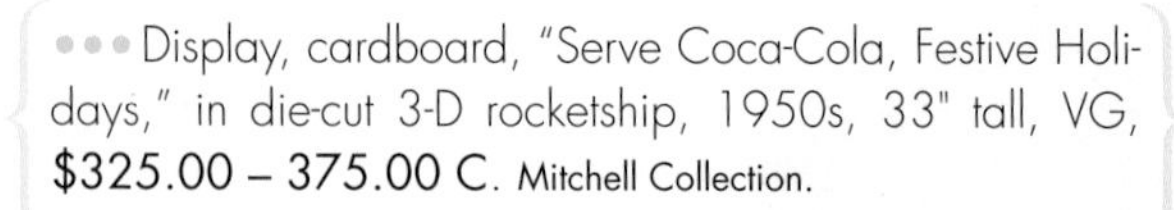

••• Display, cardboard, "Serve Coca-Cola, Festive Holidays," in die-cut 3-D rocketship, 1950s, 33" tall, VG, **$325.00 – 375.00 C.** Mitchell Collection.

••• Display, cardboard, "Things Go Better with Coke," die-cut easel back of Santa with a bottle of Coke and various scenes of people over his head, 1960s, 36" tall, EX, **$65.00 – 85.00 C**. Mitchell Collection.

••• Figurine, porcelain, animated Santa holding the book with the lists of good and bad children, EX, **$120.00 – 145.00 C**. Mitchell Collection.

••• Figurine, porcelain, Royal Orleans, limited edition, Santa standing beside a sack of toys and holding a glass of Coke, 1980s, EX, **$165.00 – 185.00 C**. Mitchell Collection.

••• Figurine, porcelain, Royal Orleans, Santa and boy with dog, 1980s, EX, **$140.00 – 155.00 C**. Mitchell Collection.

Certificate of Authenticity
Royal Orleans
is proud to present
Coca-Cola
The Classic Santa Claus
First Annual Christmas 1983

••• Figurine, porcelain, Royal Orleans, Santa with a globe and bottle of Coke, complete set contains six figures, 1980s, EX, **$200.00 – 225.00 C**. Mitchell Collection.

••• Poster, cardboard, "Coca-Cola...Christmas Greetings," Santa with bottle of Coke and note left for him by child, 1932, NM, **$4,200.00 B**. Gary Metz.

••• Poster, cardboard, "Drink Coca-Cola...Delicious and Refreshing," Santa holding a bottle of Coke, 1940s, 43" x 32", EX, **$1,000.00 B**. Gary Metz.

••• Poster, cardboard, "Take Home Coca-Cola Santa Packs," price area at right of Santa, NOS, NM, **$30.00 – 45.00 C**.

••• Sign, cardboard, "Add Zest to the Season," string hanger with Santa and a bottle of Coke, Canadian, 1949, 10½" x 18½", EX, **$900.00 B**. Gary Metz.

••• Sign, cardboard, "Coke Adds Life to Holiday Fun," Santa holding a bottle of Coke, 1960s, EX, **$100.00 – 115.00 C**.

••• Sign, cardboard, "Santa's Helpers," Santa with six bottles, 1950s, VG, **$125.00 – 150.00 C**. Mitchell Collection.

Sign, cardboard, "Sign of Good Taste...Anytime," Santa drinking from a bottle of Coke, EX, **$95.00 – 145.00 C.** Gary Metz.

Sign, cardboard, "Things Go Better with Coke," string hanger with couple kissing under mistletoe, 13½" x 16", EX, **$75.00 – 90.00 C.** Mitchell Collection.

Ad, paper, "Come In — Have a Coke," framed, under glass, EX, **$175.00 – 200.00 C.** Mitchell Collection.

Ad, paper, "Travel Refreshed," back cover of ***National Geographic***, Santa and Sprite Boy with bottle of Coke, 1949, $6\frac{7}{8}$" x 10", G, **$10.00 – 15.00 C.**

Ad, paper, "Where There's Coca-Cola There's Hospitality," with Santa looking in refrigerator, 1948, EX, **$40.00 C.**

Sprite Boy

••• Bag holder, metal, "For Home Refreshment...Coca-Cola," 36" x 17", VG, **$695.00 D – 750.00 C**.

••• Blotter, cardboard, "Good," bottle of Coke in snowbank, 7¼" x 3½", EX, **$40.00 – 55.00 C**.

••• Decal, vinyl, "Take Home a Carton," unused, framed under glass, Sprite Boy with bottle cap hat, 1940s, 8" x 10", EX, **$250.00 B**. Gary Metz.

••• Fan, cardboard, "A Way to Win... Wherever You Go," on paddle stick from the Mt. Vernon, Illinois, bottler, 1950s, EX, **$115.00 – 125.00 C**. Mitchell Collection.

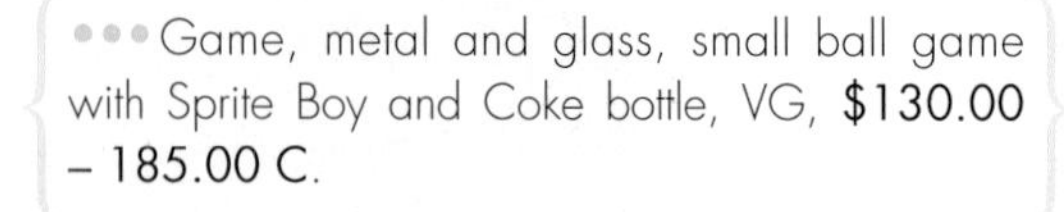

••• Game, metal and glass, small ball game with Sprite Boy and Coke bottle, VG, **$130.00 – 185.00 C**.

••• Sign, cardboard, Coca-Cola six pack, "Serve Coke at Home," Sprite Boy in bottle cap hat, 1946, 30" x 50", EX, **$600.00 C**. Gary Metz.

••• Sign, cardboard, Coca-Cola six-pack with bottle cap Sprite Boy, 34" x 43", G, **$375.00 – 425.00 C**.

••• Sign, cardboard, die-cut concession stand, part of larger sign, bottle cap Sprite Boy, 37½" x 29", EX, **$265.00 – 295.00 C**. Gary Metz.

••• Sign, Masonite and metal, "Sundaes...Malts," beautiful Kay Displays wings with center 12" button and Sprite Boy and bottle at each end, 1950s, 78" x 12", EX, **$1,050.00 B**. Gary Metz.

Sign, Masonite, "Beverage Department," featuring a "Drink..." button in center of wings and Sprite Boy on each end, Kay Displays, 1940s, 78" x 12", EX, **$850.00 B – 1,000.00 C**. Gary Metz.

Sign, metal, "Drink Coca-Cola," horizontal, with Sprite Boy and bottle in yellow spotlight, 57" x 18", VG, **$595.00 D**.

Sign, paper, "Come In...We Have Coca-Cola...5¢," line of marching glasses and Sprite Boy, 1944, 25" x 8", VG, **$350.00 B**. Gary Metz.

Sign, wood, "Welcome Friend...Have a Coke," die cut with Sprite Boy and a bottle of Coke, 1940, 32" x 14", EX, **$595.00 – 695.00 C**. Mitchell Collection.

Dispensers

Countertop, ceramic, "Coca-Cola," early soda fountain syrup dispenser from the Wheeling Pottery Co., 1896, VG, **$5,500.00 B**. Gary Metz.

Countertop, metal and plastic, "Drink Coca-Cola" painted on side, salesman's sample with fabric zippered carrying case, three heads, 1960s, EX, **$975.00 C**.

Countertop, metal, "Drink Coca-Cola," single spigot with lift top by Dole, 14½" x 11½" x 25", G, **$675.00 B**. Gary Metz.

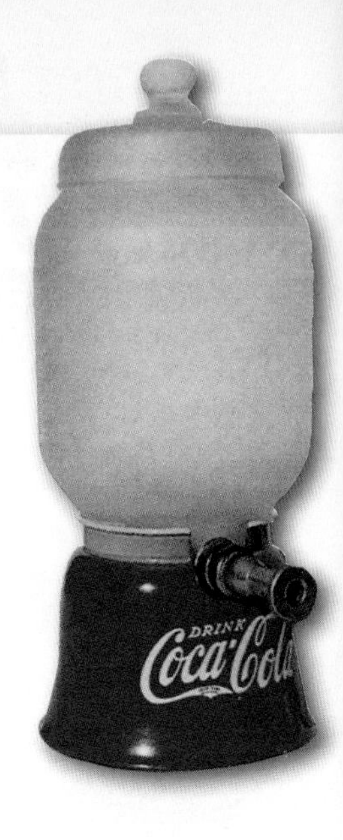

••• Countertop, porcelain and glass, "Drink Coca-Cola," frosted glass lid and top section, red pottery base, 1920s, NM, **$6,200.00 B**. Gary Metz.

••• Toy, plastic, in shape of single-spout dispenser, "Drink Coca-Cola," 1950s, EX, **$175.00 – 210.00 C**. Mitchell Collection.

••• Toy, plastic, "Things Go Better with Coke," with all original items including glasses, 1970s, VG, **$90.00 – 125.00 C**. Gary Metz.

Coca-Cola Collector's Club Items

Bottle, glass, "The Coca-Cola Collectors Club, Colorado Springs – 1997, 23rd Annual Convention," 1997, EX, **$45.00 – 55.00 C**.

Bottle, glass, "The Coca-Cola Collectors Club, July 13 – 16, 1994, 20th National Convention, Atlanta, GA," 8 oz., 1994, **$50.00 – 60.00. C**.

Bottle, glass, "Coca-Cola Collectors Club Smoky Mountain Chapter, Smoky Fest 93, May 13, 14, 15, Gatlinburg, TN," 8 oz., 1993, EX, **$40.00 – 50.00 C**.

●●● Bottle, glass, "Kansas City, 1981 Cola Clan National Convention," 10 oz., full, 1981, EX, **$50.00 – 75.00 C.**

●●● Drinking glass, flare, "Atlanta Cola Clan Welcomes You to the Third Collectors Weekend, April 13 – 15, 1979," flare style, EX, **$30.00 – 40.00 C.**

●●● Playing cards, plastic, "20th Annual Convention, the Coca-Cola Collectors Club, Atlanta, GA," 1994, NRFB, **$15.00 – 20.00 C.**

●●● Playing cards, plastic, "25th Annual Convention, the Coca-Cola Collectors Club, 1999," in original box, EX, **$10.00 – 20.00 C.**

••• Playing cards, plastic, "Badger Spring Pause, May 18 – 20, 2000," NRFB, 2000, **$15.00 – 20.00 C.**

••• Playing cards, plastic, "Coca-Cola Collectors Club, Kansas City, July 1995," EX, **$10.00 – 12.00 C.**

••• Playing cards, plastic, "Dearborn, MI, July 28th – July 31st, 1993," original box, EX, **$15.00 – 20.00 C.**

••• Playing cards, plastic, "E-Town, KY, 11th Annual Septemberfest, Sept. 17 – 19, 1987," in original box, EX, **$10.00 – 15.00 C**.

Playing cards, plastic, "12th Annual Septemberfest, E-town, KY, Sept 15 – 17, 1988," EX, **$10.00 – 15.00 C**.

Playing cards, plastic, "13th Annual Septemberfest, E-town, KY, Sept. 14 – 16, 1999," in original box, EX, **$10.00 – 15.00 C.**

Playing cards, plastic, "14th Annual Septemberfest, E-town, KY, Sept 13 – 15, 1990," in original box, EX, **$9.00 – 12.00 C**.

Playing cards, plastic, "15th Annual Septemberfest, E-Town, KY, September 19 – 21, 1991," in original box, EX, **$8.00 – 12.00 C**.

Playing cards, plastic, "16th Annual Septemberfest E-town, KY, September 17 – 19, 1992," in original box, EX, **$8.00 – 12.00 C**.

••• Pocket watch, "Septemberfest 98, Midsouth Chapter, The Coca-Cola Collectors Club," with original container, 1998, M, **$25.00 – 35.00 C.**

••• Stem goblet, glass, "The Coca-Cola Collectors Club 25th Annual Convention, Dallas, 1999," 3$\frac{3}{4}$"h x 2 $\frac{5}{16}$"w, EX, **$45.00 – 55.00 C.**

••• Tape measure, metal, "Midsouth Chapter of the Coca-Cola Collectors Club, Septemberfest, 1997," in original box, M, **$10.00 – 15.00 C.**

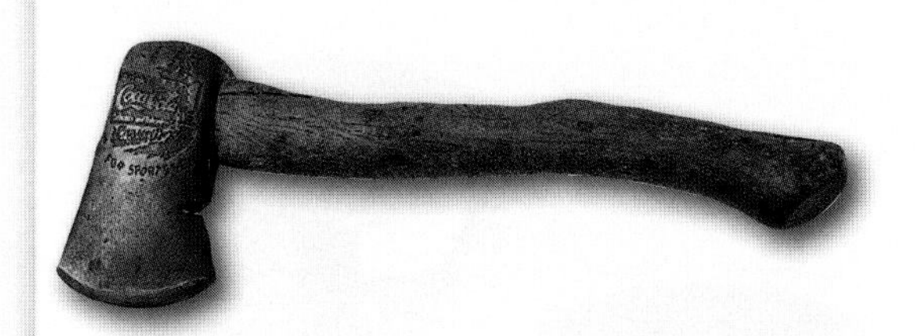

Axe, metal and wood, "Drink Coca-Cola...For Sportsmen," 1930, EX, **$950.00 – 1,300.00 C**.

Bench, wooden, "Drink Coca-Cola...," the rest is somewhat obscured, but probably says "In Bottles," 1940 – 1950s, F, **$850.00 B**.

Bookmark, celluoid, "Refreshing... Drink Coca-Cola...Delicious 5¢," 1900s, 2" x 2¼", EX, **$750.00 – 1,000.00 C**.

••• Bookmark, paper, "Drink Coca-Cola 5¢," 2" x 6", EX, $400.00 – 475.00 C.

••• Bottle lamp, composition, "Coca-Cola," brass base, rare and highly desirable, 1920s, 20" tall, NM, $7,200.00 B.

••• Bowl, china, "Drink Coca-Cola... Ice Cold," scalloped-edge Vernonware, green, 1930s, EX, $450.00 B.

••• Camera, plastic, "Coke Adds Life to Happy Times," Polaroid camera, EX, $75.00 – 125.00 C.

●●● Coupons, paper, "Take Time Out for the Pause That Refreshes," uncut sheet, EX, **$20.00 – 35.00 C**.

●●● Display counter box, cardboard, "Coca-Cola Chewing Gum," originally held twenty 5¢ packages of chewing gum, 1920s, VG, **$1,500.00 – 2,000.00 C**.

●●● Door lock, metal, "Drink Coca-Cola in Bottles Delicious and Refreshing," 1930s, EX, **$75.00 – 100.00 C**.

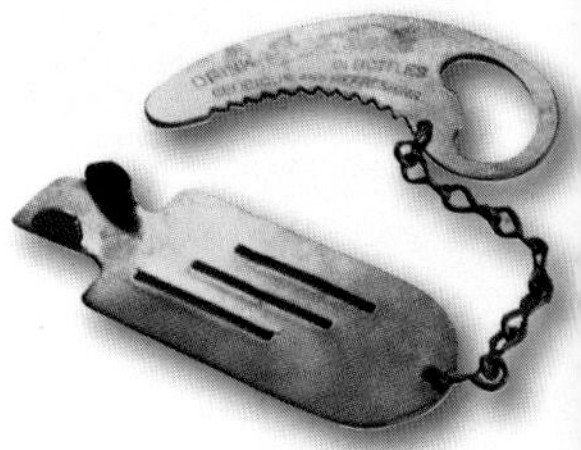

●●● License plate attachment, metal, "Aloysius Purple Flashes," 11" x 4", EX, **$150.00 B**. Buffalo Bay Auction Co.

••• Light globe, glass, "Coca-Cola 5¢," rectangular with glass, bead fringe around bottom, "Pittsburg Mosaic Glass Co., Inc., Pittsburg, Pa.," 1910, 11" x 22" x 7¼", EX, **$12,000.00 – 14,000.00 C**.

••• Light globe, glass, "Coca-Cola," schoolhouse design with original hardware, 1930s, EX, **$1,300.00 – 1,575.00 C**.

••• Light globe, glass, "Drink Coca-Cola," 1930 – 1940s, EX, **$400.00 – 500.00 C**.

••• Napkin holder, metal, "Drink Coca-Cola," foreign, resembles a box-type cooler, 1940s, F, **$525.00 B**.

••• Note pad, celluloid, "Drink Coca-Cola in Bottles," 1920s, EX, **$900.00 B**.

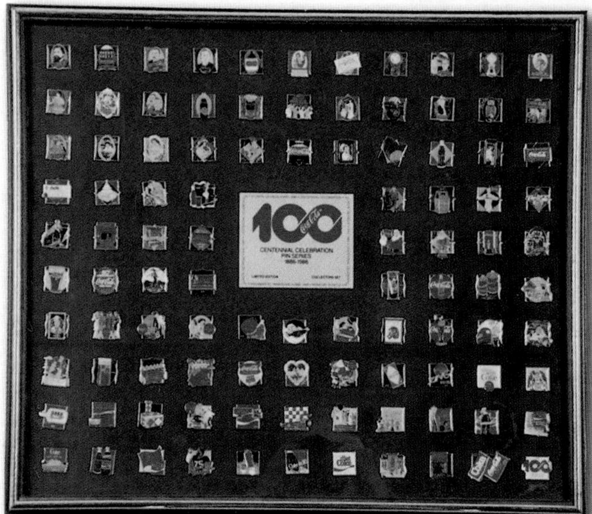

••• Pin set, metal and wood, "100 Centennial Celebration Pin Series," in framed presentation box, 1986, EX, **$300.00 – 400.00 C**.

••• Record holder, plastic, "Hi-Fi," premium for 45 rpm records on revolving base, 10" x 10¾", NM, **$100.00 B – 125.00 C**.

••• Record set, vinyl and cardboard, "Got a Long Thirst?...Get a Long King!" record and 45 rpm autographed by Ricky Nelson, this is difficult to find and of course crosses collecting lines, so it's very much in demand, 1960s, 18" x 14½", G, **$575.00** B.

••• Straws, cardboard box, "Be Really Refreshed...Drink Coca-Cola," with fishtail logo, 1960s, EX, **$250.00** B.

••• Street marker, brass, "Drink Coca-Cola... Safety First," very collectible item, these were originally used to mark crosswalks at schools, 1920s, VG, **$150.00 – 225.00** C.

••• String holder, metal, "Take Home Coca-Cola in Cartons," yellow spotlight with carton, 1930s, 14" x 16", EX, **$1,000.00** B.

B.J. Summers' Guide to
Coca-Cola
SIXTH EDITION

B.J. Summers' Guide to
Coca-Cola
SIXTH EDITION
Identifications
Current Values
Buvez Coca-Cola
La Soif n'a pas de saison
COKE BELONGS
SERVE COKE AT HOME
TAKE SOME HOME
Coca-Cola
DRINK Coca-Cola

The Museum has the only complete classic Coca-Cola serving tray collection known to exist.

The 32,000 square foot facility houses rotating exhibits of the Schmidt Museum Collection which contains over 80,000 items. The facility features a larger museum store and visitor comforts along with expanded displays and exhibits, historic vehicles, a turn-of-the-century bottling plant exhibit, neon sign displays, vending machines, and of course the only complete serving tray collection known to exist. Anything and everything with a Coca-Cola trademark is on display!

THE WORLD'S LARGEST PRIVATE COLLECTION
COCA-COLA
ANTIQUES, ARTIFACTS, AND COLLECTIBLES

Schmidt Museum of Coca-Cola Memorabilia
109 Buffalo Creek Drive
Elizabethtown, KY 42701
Phone – (270) 234-1100
E-mail: schmidtmuseum@yahoo.com

This Museum is a non-profit entity which is neither owned by nor affiliated with the Coca-Cola Company.

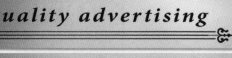

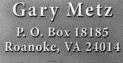

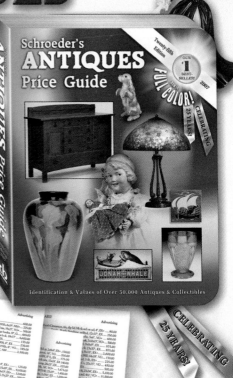